Writing for Social Work

Sara Miller McCune founded SAGE Publishing in 1965 to support the dissemination of usable knowledge and educate a global community. SAGE publishes more than 1000 journals and over 800 new books each year, spanning a wide range of subject areas. Our growing selection of library products includes archives, data, case studies and video. SAGE remains majority owned by our founder and after her lifetime will become owned by a charitable trust that secures the company's continued independence.

Los Angeles | London | New Delhi | Singapore | Washington DC | Melbourne

Writing for Social Work

Lucy Rai

Learning Matters

Learning Matters
A SAGE Publishing Company
1 Oliver's Yard
55 City Road
London EC1Y 1SP

SAGE Publications Inc.
2455 Teller Road
Thousand Oaks, California 91320

SAGE Publications India Pvt Ltd
B 1/I 1 Mohan Cooperative Industrial Area
Mathura Road
New Delhi 110 044

SAGE Asia-Pacific Pte Ltd
3 Church Street
#10–04 Samsung Hub
Singapore 049483

Editor: Kate Keers
Development editor: Sarah Turpie
Senior project editor: Chris Marke
Project management: Deer Park Productions
Marketing manager: Camille Richmond
Cover design: Wendy Scott
Typeset by: C&M Digitals (P) Ltd, Chennai, India

Library of Congress Control Number: 2020951405

British Library Cataloguing in Publication Data

A catalogue record for this book is available from
the British Library

ISBN 978-1-5264-7634-0
ISBN 978-1-5264-7635-7 (pbk)

Contents

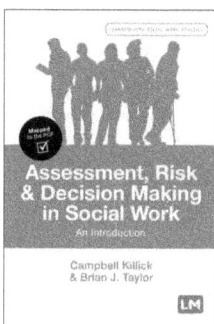

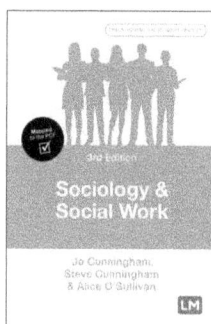

Acknowledgements

This book draws on almost two decades of research into writing in social work, a journey I have travelled with Theresa Lillis, initially as my PhD supervisor and latterly as a co-researcher and friend. Theresa has been a valued mentor and her commitment to social justice alongside unfailing academic rigour has been and continues to be an inspiration to me. This book would not exist without her support, insight and wise counsel over many years.

I would also like to thank all of the research participants and students over the years who have in many ways helped me to listen and understand the experiences of learning to write at university and in social work practice. Their voices are at the heart of this book and I hope that readers' own experiences will in turn enrich the value of the chapters that follow.

Chapter 5 was written with the help of Debbie Holmes from PebblePad and I would like to thank her for her time and patience in working with me to develop this chapter.

The poem used in Chapter 10, 'Holding On', has been included with the kind permission of Lucy Berry. I came across this poem many years ago and the words have stayed with me as a powerful reflection of the feelings I had as my sons grew into independent adulthood. My sincere thanks to Lucy for helping me to track down the original version and giving permission for it to be included in this book.

Finally, books only come to life with the support and encouragement of friends and family and I would particularly like to thank Sheila Finlayson, Italo Cadamuro and Steve Meade.

About the author

Lucy Rai is a senior lecturer in social work at the Open University and also Director of PRAXIS, the Scholarship Centre for the Faculty of Wellbeing, Education and Language Studies. Lucy has been researching social work writing since 2012 and has published widely on the subject of academic writing in social work. Lucy began her career as a qualified social worker, primarily working with children and families, and has been teaching social work since 1995. Lucy was the chair of the Impact Advisory Group for the ESRC-funded *Writing in Social Work* research project and is author of *Professional Writing in Social Work: Making a Difference* (2014) and 'Writing skills for social workers', in J. Parker (ed.), *Introducing Social Work* (2020). Lucy is a Principal Fellow of the Higher Education Authority, now Advance HE.

* * *

This book also includes two chapters co-authored with **Theresa Lillis**. Theresa is Professor Emeritus of English Language and Applied Linguistics at the Open University, UK. Her writing research centres on academic and professional writing about which she has published extensively, including *Academic Writing in a Global Context* (Routledge, 2010), *The Sociolinguistics of Writing* (EUP, 2013) and articles on social work writing in the journals, *Journal of Applied Linguistics and Professional Practice, Text and Talk* and *Written Communication*. She is the Principal Investigator of the first nationally-funded project on social work writing, *Writing in Professional Social Work Practice in a Changing Communicative Landscape* (WiSP http://www.writinginsocialwork.com).

Series editor's preface

During recent teaching sessions for student social workers I have been struck keenly by the changes permeating our contemporary world. Values and ethics lie at the heart of social work and social work education, and we address these throughout all the books in the series. The positions that we take in terms of values and ethics is, to an extent, determined by context, time and experience and these are expressed in different ways by students coming into social work education today.

Since the turn of this century we have witnessed shifts and challenges as the marketised neoliberal landscape of politics, economy and social life may attract little comment or contest from some. We have observed the political machinery directing much of statutory social work towards a focus on individuals apart from their environment. However, we have also seen a new turn to the social in the #MeToo campaign where unquestioned entitlement to women's bodies and psychology is exposed and resisted. We have seen defiance of those perpetuating social injustices that see long-term migrants alongside today's migrants abused and shunned by society, institutions as well as individuals. Questioning the status quo in social and public policy assumed greater significance during the Covid-19 pandemic in which damage to health and social care wrought by ten years of austerity measures were clearly exposed. We stand at a time in which social policy and the well-being of others are seen as priorities, and the work of social workers is recognised as a key service.

It is likely that, as a student of social work, you will lay bare and face many previously unquestioned assumptions, which can be very perplexing and uncover needs for learning, support and understanding. This series of books acts as an aid as you make these steps. Each book stands in a long and international tradition of social work that promotes social justice and human rights, introducing you to the importance of sometimes new and difficult concepts, and inculcating the importance of close questioning of yourself as you make your journey towards becoming part of that tradition.

There are numerous contemporary challenges for the wider world, and for all four countries of the UK. These include political shifts to the 'popular' Right, a growing antipathy to care and support, and dealing with lies and 'alternative truths' in our daily lives. Alongside this, is the need to address the impact of an increasingly ageing population with its attendant social care needs and working with the financial implications that such a changing demography brings. At the other end of the lifespan the need for high-quality childcare, welfare and safeguarding services has been highlighted as society develops and responds to the changing complexion. As demand rises so do the costs and the unquestioned assumption that austerity measures are necessary continues to create tensions and restrictions in services, policies and expectations.

As a social worker you will work with a diverse range of people throughout your career, many of whom have experienced significant, even traumatic, events that require a professional and caring response. As well as working with individuals, however, you may be required to respond to the needs of a particular community disadvantaged by local, national or world events or groups excluded within their local communities because of assumptions made about them.

The importance of high-quality social work education remains if we are adequately to address the complexities of modern life. We should continually strive for excellence in education as this allows us to focus clearly on what knowledge it is useful to engage with when learning to be a social worker. Questioning everything, especially from a position of knowledge is central to being a social worker.

The books in this series respond to the agendas driven by changes brought about by professional bodies, governments and disciplinary reviews. They aim to build on and offer introductory texts based on up-to-date knowledge and to help communicate this in an accessible way, so preparing the ground for future study and for encouraging good practice as you develop your social work career. Each book is written by someone passionate about social work and social services and aims to instil that passion in others.

Social workers engage in constant communication using a wide array of media to do so. Lucy Rai's book immerses you into the professional practice of social work writing with its specific audiences, the need for particular foci, styles and nuances, and its centrality to good practice. This is something you will engage with throughout your career and begins now in your learning for practice. The current text offers a grounding from which to enhance your learning and to understand the communicative and relational aspects of professional social work writing. By using the CAPS model, focusing on context, audience, purpose and self, Rai gives you a framework to develop effective writing in your practice.

Professor Jonathan Parker

January 2021

Introduction

Research suggests that social workers can spend between 50 and 98 per cent of their time writing (Lillis et al., 2020). The writing that they do is highly significant, having an impact on decisions about, for example, removal of liberty, provision of services and allocation of funding. Social work students, in common with students across higher education, are heavily assessed through writing. This reliance on writing is despite the substantial practice element of assessment because evidence of practice competence still requires written texts, for example in the form of practice portfolios and writing undertaken in practice. It is for this reason that writing has been described as a 'high stakes activity' for both students and social workers (Lillis, 2017; Lillis and Tuck, 2016; Rai, 2014; Lillis and Rai, 2011). The judgement on whether a student passes and qualifies as a social worker, therefore, relies not only on their practice competence but on the effectiveness of their writing as a student and a practitioner.

This book is underpinned by research into social work writing pre- and post-qualification (Rai, 2004, 2006, 2008, 2014; Rai and Lillis, 2012; Lillis, 2001, 2010, 2017). You will encounter Research Summaries throughout the book which will outline a range of research sources that are drawn upon. Chapters 7 and 8 have been co-written with Professor Theresa Lillis who led the research project *Writing in Professional Social Work Practice* (WiSP) funded by the Economic and Social Research Council (ESRC ES/M008703/1). Data from WiSP has been used to create authentic case studies in Chapters 7, 8 and 9 (data from WiSP is available at the UK Data Service Repository). Additional case studies have been developed based on both my own doctoral research and practice experience as a qualified social worker. The book includes examples relevant to working with a range of service user groups, including children and families, older people, disabled people and young people involved in crime. The approach across the book is to enable you to apply your learning to your own studies and practice through activities and case studies.

Book structure

Part One Academic and assessed writing

Chapter 1 outlines the core theoretical approach of the book and introduces readers to 'CAPS', a simple mnemonic used to help writers to reflect on how to approach new writing tasks through a consideration of the **C**ontext, **A**udience, **P**urpose and **S**elf.

Part One of *Writing for Social Work* focuses on academic and assessed writing at university. It begins with *Chapter 2*, which introduces academic writing and how to use guidance on assessed work. The rest of Part One explores specific kinds of writing in some depth.

Chapter 3 focuses on writing essays, which are one of the most common forms of academic assessment. You will learn some techniques for planning your essay, including gathering evidence and constructing an effective argument.

Chapter 4 turns to reflective writing, a particularly important form of writing in social work and other practice-based disciplines. The differences between, and overlaps with, essays are explored and CAPS is used to illustrate how to interrogate assignment tasks.

Chapter 5 focuses on writing about practice, for example creating portfolios, and addresses the important challenge of applying theory to practice.

Part One concludes with *Chapter 6* which explores writing about research, both as a student and in practice. This chapter provides examples of the kinds of research social workers may be involved in writing about, the elements that should be included in an effective research report and how to evaluate research.

Part Two Writing in social work practice

In Part Two we turn to writing in social work practice. These chapters will be of particular value to students on practice placements and recently qualified practitioners. Part Two begins with *Chapter 7* on case recording, which is perhaps the writing task that social workers spend most time on.

This is followed by two closely related chapters, *Chapter 8* which covers reports for assessment and reviews while *Chapter 9* covers report writing for court. In all of these chapters you will have the opportunity to read authentic case studies from practice based on research and apply the CAPS mnemonic to plan your own writing tasks.

The final chapter of the book, *Chapter 10*, explores therapeutic writing. This is a very different use of writing from those covered in the book this far, and it includes creating rich pictures which involve drawings and diagrams as well as words. This final chapter also considers the ways in which writing can be therapeutic when working with service users as well as in your own professional development.

Achieving a social work degree

This book will help you develop the following social work capabilities from the *Professional Capabilities Framework* (PCF) (BASW, 2018). The PCF sets out the values, knowledge and skills that social workers should command at different levels of experience, including student social workers and those who are newly qualified.

Knowledge – Develop and apply relevant knowledge from social work practice and research, sciences, law, other professional and relevant fields, and from the experience of people who use services.

Critical reflection and analysis – Apply critical reflection and analysis to inform and provide a rationale for professional decision-making

Skills and interventions – Use judgement, knowledge and authority to intervene with individuals, families and communities to provide support, prevent harm and enable progress

See Appendix 1 for the Professional Capabilities Framework Fan and a description of the nine domains.

It will also introduce you to the following standards as set out in the Social Work Subject Benchmark Statement (2019):

Problem-solving skills

5.12 Gathering information: graduates in social work are able to:

     i. demonstrate persistence in gathering information from a wide range of sources and

     ii. using a variety of methods, for a range of purposes. These methods include

     iii. electronic searches, reviews of relevant literature, policy and procedures, face-to-face

     iv. interviews, and written and telephone contact with individuals and groups take into account differences of viewpoint in gathering information and critically

     v. assess the reliability and relevance of the information gathered

     vi. assimilate and disseminate relevant information in reports and case records

Communication skills

5.15 Graduates in social work are able to communicate clearly, sensitively and effectively (using appropriate methods which may include working with interpreters) with individuals and groups of different ages and abilities in a range of formal and informal situations, in order to:

     i. engage individuals and organisations, who may be unwilling, by verbal, paper-based and electronic means to achieve a range of objectives, including changing behaviour

     ii. use verbal and non-verbal cues to guide and inform conversations and interpretation of information

     iii. negotiate and, where necessary, redefine the purpose of interactions with individuals and organisations and the boundaries of their involvement

     iv. listen actively and empathetically to others, taking into account their specific needs and life experiences

     v. engage appropriately with the life experiences of service users, to understand accurately their viewpoint, overcome personal prejudices and respond appropriately to a range of complex personal and interpersonal situations

     vi. make evidence-informed arguments drawing from theory, research and practice wisdom, including the viewpoints of service users and/or others

     vii. write accurately and clearly in styles adapted to the audience, purpose and context of the communication

     viii. use advocacy skills to promote others' rights, interests and needs

Subject-specific skills and other skills

See Appendix 2 for a detailed description of these standards

1

How to be an effective writer

Introduction

In Chapter 1 you will consider who you are as a writer. What is the experience that you bring to your writing and what are the ways in which your past experiences can have an impact on how you write? You will explore the assignment guidance that you will encounter on your course and how you should interpret this when you write academic assessments. You will also consider the conventions, or expectations, of writing at university and how to develop your writing to meet these expectations. Social work is a relatively new academic discipline and we will explore the implications of this for your academic writing. Finally you will learn about the CAPS model, which will be used throughout this book to help you reflect and understand what different kinds of writing require of you.

Who are you as a writer?

When you think about writing what comes to mind? What memories does learning to write evoke for you? Throughout this book I will ask you to pause and do some thinking and writing. You might like to set up a file or find a notebook to keep your writing in so that you can look back on your notes. The reason for these tasks is to help you learn about writing in the particular context that is relevant to you. For example, these first two related writing tasks arise from the fact that writing, like all forms of communication, is very individual and to develop your own writing you need to understand how your history and identity has shaped you as a writer.

Activity 1.1   Your language history

Read the following prompt questions and then write for about 10 minutes. Try to keep writing and if you get stuck turn to one of the other questions to get you moving again. Once you have finished, read your writing back to yourself and then find someone to share it with – this could be a tutor, fellow student, colleague or friend.

1. What language(s) do you speak at home? Was this the first language you learnt?
2. Do you speak any other languages or dialects? By dialect I mean different ways of talking within one language, so may refer to differences in pronunciation, accent or words used.
3. You may consider that you only speak one language fluently, but that the way in which you talk changes depending on who you are talking to.
4. Where or with whom would you use a particular language or dialect? Think about family, friends, education contexts and work.
5. Your choice of language or dialect in a particular context might be unconscious, but reflecting on it now, why do you think you change the way that you speak in each context?

Comment

Language is very important – it contributes to forming our identity and is also an expression of who we are. Language connects us with other people but can also isolate and exclude us from particular social groups. Writing in contexts like university and social work practice in the UK are generally expected to be based on a particular form of English, sometimes referred to as 'Standard English', which is significantly different from the way in which most people speak, even if English is their first language. Trudgill and Hannah suggest that only 15 per cent of the population in the UK would speak Standard English as their native dialect. Like all languages, English is organic in that not only does it have many varieties but changes over time. Standard English has no inherent superiority in terms of expression or clarity of meaning. It evolved from the language preferred by the governing and upper classes and then became standardised and stabilised over time, due to it being committed to print (Trudgill and Hannah, 2013). Standard English continues to be important as it is the basis of writing undertaken in schools, universities and many other formal contexts including social work. Familiarity with Standard English, therefore, can give you an advantage when learning to write in any of these contexts.

Activity 1.2   Your writing history

As with the previous writing exercise, read the prompts and then try to keep writing for ten minutes – if you get stuck go back to one of the other questions. Once you have finished, read your writing back to yourself and then find someone to share it with but this time try and talk to someone who knew you as a child and ask if they have any other memories of you as a writer.

1.   What do you remember about learning to write?
2.   Do you have any particularly positive or negative memories? What were they?
3.   Can you think of any teacher comments about your writing?
4.   Did you enjoy writing or was it something you struggled with?
5.   Did you write outside school? For example did you keep a diary, communicating with friends in writing or maybe you wrote creatively such as stories or poems? When you wrote outside of school did you write differently?
6.   As you grew up, did anything change about how you felt about yourself as a writer?

For some people the memories stimulated by these questions might be difficult or uncomfortable; for others these exercise might seem irrelevant. The following two case studies are adapted from real experiences of students who participated in research into social work student writing (Rai, 2008) and illustrate how powerful language and writing histories can be, and how they can influence our development as writers.

Case Study

Alisha

I was born in Jamaica but came to live with my grandparents when I was six. In Jamaica and at home with my parents I spoke Patois, I still use it with many of my friends and with family as it is the language that I am most comfortable with. It depends who I am talking with though, with some people I might use more London English but the odd word of Patois. In school I had to learn to speak differently and I remember it being hard to write when I first came to the UK. Lots of us Black kids were put in special needs groups because of our writing, but we missed out because teachers assumed we were not academic, but I wanted to read and learn. Our house was full of books and my grandparents and parents wanted me to do well in school. It was hard though because it wasn't just that I would use different words and have an accent, the grammar is different too, like the word order, so I had to work hard to learn to write in Standard English. I was also confused when I heard people say Patois isn't a language, it's just broken or bad English. I now understand more about where Jamaican Patois came from, how it developed from many languages. I am proud of it now, but as a child I felt embarrassed and even stupid at times. I still feel more 'me'

(Continued)

(Continued)

speaking in Patios or with bits of Patios, but I would never use it at work or at uni. That makes it hard it do the reflective writing as I don't really feel as if I am writing as me, I have to think myself into someone else, the kind of professional me.

Case Study

Mark

I found a school report tucked away in a drawer. It said 'Mark is an able child until he puts pen to paper.' Even 40 years later that comment stung and brought back the hurt and humiliation I felt at school. I had lots of ideas, I enjoyed learning and I was always a very active participant in class. I actually also enjoyed writing, but my spelling was always poor and so my marks for written work were never good. Teachers' comments were that my written work was lazy and careless. As a child I assumed this to be true, and also that I just wasn't very bright. Looking back now I see things differently. I gained a degree and a master's, so I don't think I lack intellectual ability. What changed was that my spelling became less of an issue when I began to routinely write on computers with spell checkers. I am also now aware that both of my parents, one of whom qualified in medicine from Cambridge, and two other close family members also struggled with spelling. I don't think we were all careless and lazy so assume there could be an inherited problem, mild enough not to have seriously affected learning to read but enough to make spelling a struggle. The real impact on me was that for much of my adult life I have felt an imposter in the academic world. As a social worker I found numerous strategies to avoid writing in public unless it was mediated through a computer. The writing that I really enjoyed as a child was the writing that was just for me, like diaries I kept as a teenager. I do now also enjoy writing professionally, but only because I am less worried about getting caught out and judged for my poor spelling.

Comment

Mark and Alisha's reflections may have some resonance for you, or your experience may be very different. Whatever your own language and writing reflections they will have influenced your experiences as a writer and for some people such reflections can help you to understand and resolve writing difficulties that you encounter. One of the important lessons from such reflections is that the ability to write effectively relies on more than just the structure or surface features of written language, such as spelling, grammar and punctuation. Also, learning these surface features does not take place on a level playing field, it can be much more challenging for some people depending on a range of individual factors. Mark may have mild dyslexia which was never tested for or diagnosed but given his family history this may have explained his difficulty with spelling. Regardless of the cause, spelling was a challenge and this got in the way of Mark's ability to be a confident learner and also caused anxieties writing as a mature student and professional.

Alisha's experiences are not unusual. In my early career teaching in higher education I was asked to provide a study skills session for social workers who had all been referred due to concerns about their writing. I arrived at the session prepared to teach grammar. The experience I had over the following hour changed my career and stimulated a commitment to researching and understanding student writing in social work. The group were all women, all social work students and all shared a Caribbean heritage. All moved to the UK as young children, most from Jamaica but some also from the Dominican Republic and St Lucia. Rather than teaching grammar I listened. These women told me about how speaking Patois or Creole at home made them feel and how they felt about changing how they talked when at work, on placement and at university. They told me the Patois they spoke at home reflected history and how this history is evident in the structure and vocabulary of the languages. Most strikingly they explained how switching languages meant they needed to leave part of their identity at home, there seemed to be no place for it in their writing. I learnt a lot more from this group of students than they learnt from me, but this experience set me on a research journey which is reflected in this book. It convinced me that while learning the structure of written English is important, it is only one element of being an effective writer.

Learning the 'rules of the game'

Learning to write successfully in higher education can be a frustrating process. Students can feel confused and demoralised as they try to weave their way through the expectations of their university, course and tutors. Writing in higher education is not a game: it involves a significant investment of time and money and students will only pass their course if they can write effectively. Lillis (2001) suggests that as the main assessment tool writing becomes a tool for gatekeeping ... *with students passing or failing courses according to the ways in which they respond to, and engage in, academic writing tasks* (Lillis, 2001, p20). The allusion to a game indicates only that writing at university is a rule-bound activity in which students can win or lose. Frustratingly there is no definitive rule book and students need to negotiate complex written and unwritten requirements in order to succeed.

Case Study

Bernie

They give you so many rules, you can't do this and you mustn't do that, you must ensure that you do this and if this is missing blah blah blah, there is so much you have to remember that you just get scared, scared that you are going to miss something out. There is so much to remember that you might miss it out ...

Bernie was just beginning her second year as a social work student at the time that she made this comment to me during a research interview. She enjoyed writing and

(Continued)

(Continued)

was an experienced practitioner before being seconded onto her qualifying course by her employer. She was looking forward to her studies but quickly became demoralised when she began writing her assignments and receiving feedback. Despite reading all of the guidance carefully she found it confusing. The guidance was provided in so many places, each module had an assessment guide, there was a programme assessment document and the university also published assessment regulations. Bernie's first-level module also contained study skills teaching on writing and she had been directed to generic toolkits provided by the library. After her first course she thought she had familiarised herself with all of this information and she got a good mark on her year one assessments. She was devastated on getting a poor mark on her first second year essay after applying all of the advice and guidance, including feedback from her first year tutor. She felt like the rules had been changed and her confidence was shaken to the point that she found it very hard to begin writing any more assignments.

Comment

Bernie's experiences reflect some of the challenges for students in their writing. Bernie did not have particular difficulties with her competence in using written English, such as spelling, grammar and punctuation. The difficulties she faced arose from interpreting and applying the range of guidance on her course and her discovery that the expectations on one module differed from those on another. Bernie assumed that having succeeded on one module she could apply all of the same 'rules' to subsequent modules and receive similarly good marks. There are many reasons why Bernie may have received a lower mark for her assignment in her second module, but one explanation could be the differences in assessment requirements between different subjects within one course. The impact of inconsistent 'disciplinary conventions' are discussed below but first let us consider the sources of advice and guidance that Bernie drew on.

Support for academic writing in universities is most commonly offered through centralised learning centres, libraries or writing centres. Staff in these units may work closely with subject specialists or may offer support independently. There is a range of approaches commonly offered and these include:

- Skills development in discrete elements of written language, such as the use of grammar and punctuation.
- Development of generic study skills such as referencing, note-taking or information and digital literacy.
- Teaching generic academic style and conventions – this can include guidance on expectations around how to structure different kinds of text, appropriate vocabulary, good academic practice in the use of evidence and citations and using an appropriate 'voice'. These areas will all be discussed in more detail in the chapters that follow, so don't worry if they are not clear to you now.
- Writing within specific disciplines – although there are some broad principles of academic writing that are generic many are specific to the discipline that you are writing for. Some disciplines are relatively discrete, such as sociology, psychology or law. By this I mean that

they have developed as distinct subjects of study which do not draw on other disciplines. Social work, in comparison, is a complex subject which includes all of these disciplines and more. Again, this is discussed in more detail in the chapters that follow.

All of these approaches have a value but research undertaken into student writing has identified that it can be unhelpful for writing support to focus primarily on a 'skills approach' (Rai, 2014). This approach is based on the assumption that a writer will be successful if they are able to learn and transfer generic writing skills, such as grammar and punctuation, to all written tasks. While an ability to confidently and effectively use structural features of language such as grammar and punctuation is an important skill in the writer's toolkit, this approach has some important limitations. Firstly it is based on the assumption that effective writing relies *only* on the use of structural features. This overlooks the fact that effective writing requires much more than the correct language; for example, there are important differences across disciplines and specific writing tasks in how arguments should be constructed and knowledge used. Secondly a skills approach places responsibility for effective writing solely on the individual writer and as a result overlooks a complex range of other factors that influence the whether a piece of writing is judged to be good or bad.

Research Summary

Lillis (2001) suggests that rather than focusing on the student as a 'problem' to be fixed, there are a range of issues arising from the ways that universities assess writing and the expectations arising from the discipline and the university. Research in this field (Baynham, 2000; Horner and Lu, 1999; Lea and Street, 1998; Lillis, 1997, 2001; Street, 1984) has therefore challenged a skills approach, suggesting that it is important to think carefully about how subject specialists, policies and guidelines on writing or assessment and even some study skills support toolkits might contribute to the challenge of producing an effective text. This approach, referred to as the social practices approach, encourages educators to take a critical view on the guidance, support, assessment strategies and marking practices used in order to reflect on the ways in which these might contribute to the success or challenges experienced by students.

Note: The terminology may vary across universities but 'course' is used here to refer to the whole qualification or programme of study which contains several 'modules'. 'Module' is used to indicate a unit of learning within one or more assessments. Modules may be referred to in some universities as 'units' or even 'courses'.

Activity 1.3   Understanding the Guidance

The following section will introduce a range of sources of advice and guidance on assignment writing.

(Continued)

(Continued)

If you are currently involved in a teaching programme as a student or educator, try and identify an example of a guidance document at each level.

1. How easy were they to find?
2. Did you find any duplication or contradictions in advice relevant to writing?

University-wide assessment regulations

It is usual for universities to provide assessment regulations that are applied across all subjects and qualifications. These regulations should inform students of the generic and minimum standards required of their writing in all assessments. Academic staff should refer to these regulations to make sure that guidance within a specific module or assignment is consistent. While this may seem straightforward, there may be a number of documents included in the overall university assessment regulations. For example, searching within my own university there are five documents relating to assessment regulations: an assessment handbook, rules on plagiarism, a code of practice for assessment, academic regulations and guidance for disabled students. This high-level documentation will include policies which would be applied if a student was considered to have breached them, such as regulations on academic conduct including plagiarism and cheating. All of these documents may have information relating to guidance on writing.

Course-wide assessment guidance

Some courses will provide guidance which is applied to all of the modules contained within it. This might be very similar to or make reference to the university guidance but also includes some elements that are specific to the course. Course-wide guidance may provide information on submission dates and procedures but it may also contain generic requirements around referencing and layout such as including the student's name and identifier. Course guides may also contain information on the assessment strategy. An assessment strategy provides information on the pass mark and the weighting for each assignment. The weighting refers to the proportion of the overall result that each assignment carries as illustrated in the following example of the first year of a course containing four modules (see Table 1.1).

Table 1.1 Example of module weighting

Module	Assignment 1	Assignment 2	Assignment 3
A	25%	25%	50%
B	20%	30%	50%
C	50%	50%	Threshold
D	90%	10%	Threshold

In this example for Module A the final grade will be determined by calculating the proportion of the overall outcome for each assessment task. Assignment 1 would contribute 25 per cent of the final mark, assignment 2 would contribute 25 per cent and assignment 3 would contribute 50 per cent. This model is the same as in Module B but with different weightings. It is important to remember that the weighting is different from the pass mark. The minimum pass mark might be set at, for example, 40 per cent for all assignments. Depending on the regulations at your university you may need to achieve a pass (more than 40 per cent) in all assignments in order to pass the module. This is not always the case and you may achieve a pass if the average of all your marks meets the minimum pass mark.

Some assignments are not given a numerical grade, for example practice placements or practical assignments which have a simple pass/fail outcome. Such pass/fail assignments or often referred to as threshold assessments, in other words students must pass them in order to pass the module. A threshold assignment will therefore not be weighted and your 'grade' is determined based on those assignments which are marked using a numerical grade. Here is an example for Modules A and C (Tables 1.2 and 1.3) which illustrate the outcome of modules with weighted assessments where all elements of the assignment must be passed.

Table 1.2 Module A (all assignments must be passed)

	Assignment 1	Assignment 2	Assignment 3	Final outcome
Weighting	25%	25%	50%	
Student 1	60%	30%	80%	Fail (without a requirement to pass all assignments the weighted grade would have been 62%)
Student 2	60%	70%	40%	Pass with 51%
Student 3	60%	60%	60%	Pass with 60%

Table 1.3 Module C (all assignments must be passed)

	Assignment 1	Assignment 2	Assignment 3	Final outcome
Weighting	50%	50%	Threshold	
Student 1	60%	30%	Pass	Fail (without a requirement to pass all assignments the weighted grade would have been 45%)
Student 2	60%	70%	Fail	Fail (without the threshold the result would have been 65%)
Student 3	60%	60%	Pass	Pass 60%

Module-specific guidance

Specific module guidance is often the most easily accessible and the starting point for many students. Module guidance may refer students out to university and course-wide documents but also contains important and specific information about how individual assignments will be assessed. Academic assignments are normally assessed against learning outcomes. Advance HE, a UK-wide organisation that sets standards for higher education, defines learning objectives as 'a statement of intention' and learning outcomes as 'a measurement of achievement' (HEA, 2019). Module-level assessment guides will also detail the assessment tasks including word limits and submission dates. They may also include extensive advice on how to write your assignment but this will vary considerably across modules, courses and universities. Some courses may provide module-wide guidance which includes assessment and also a separate document providing specific instructions for each assignment, sometimes referred to as an assessment or assignment brief.

As Bernie discovered, applying the guidance from these resources can be a challenge but some students will struggle to even find all of the information they are expected to familiarise themselves with. How easy was it for you to find examples of guidance at the university and course level? It is not uncommon for there to be duplication of information across sources, but the problem arises where there are inconsistencies. Such inconsistencies may arise from errors, but more commonly from genuine differences in requirements between assignments and modules. There are many potential reasons for such differences, some may be intentional while others are not. For example, there can be intentionally different requirements arising from specific assignment types (such as an essay, case study, report or portfolio) but inconsistencies may arise from divergent expectations of different tutors' departments responsible for drafting guidance. While this may sound alarming it arises from well recognised differences embedded in the 'conventions' of writing within individual disciplines.

Writing conventions

Academic writing conventions are the rules that govern how we are expected to write in the context of higher education. They apply to student assignments but also to writing published in books and journals. Some of these expectations are explicitly set out in written guidance, such as the assignment guidance for students discussed above or for published journal articles in the author guidelines provided by the editorial board. Table 1.4 is adapted from the list of requirements for author submission to the *British Journal of Social Work*, but most if not all of these points would be included in many undergraduate assignment guidelines:

Table 1.4 Example author guidelines

Journal author guidelines	Your own assignment guidelines?
Word length	
Referencing method	
Plagiarism policy	

Journal author guidelines	Your own assignment guidelines?
Use of literature to evidence claims	
Presentation style (word spacing, font, margins, etc.)	
Use of footnotes	
Use of appendices	
Use of key words	
Use of English (if this is the required language for submission)	
Format of figures and tables	
Layout, including use of title page and author details	
Confidentiality where data or practice is referred to	
Guidance on the use of abbreviations or acronyms	
Inclusion of critical analysis	
Structure (for example, use of introduction, conclusion and paragraphs)	
Inclusion of anti-oppressive/discriminatory perspectives	

Activity 1.4   Assignment guidance

Compare this list with the guidance on a recent assignment that you wrote or set for students. How many of these points are covered in relation to student writing?

Comment

Although it can be hard for students to navigate across guidelines on their writing, the kinds of areas listed above are normally explicitly stated. Academic writing conventions also include expectations of writing that are implicit. They do not appear in the guidelines but students can be penalised if their writing does not confirm to the expectations of the person assessing their work. These implicit expectations are also variable across individual assessors, modules, courses and universities. This can pose a challenge for students when moving between modules, courses or universities.

Research Summary

There has been considerable research into implicit academic writing conventions and the way in which these differ between disciplines or academic subjects. Lea and Stierer (2000) define academic conventions as generally accepted discipline-specific rules of writing – these include use of the first person, the structure, validity and use of evidence, the use of argument and the.rules of referencing. Inconsistencies in disciplinary writing

(Continued)

(Continued)

conventions reflect deep and significant differences in the ways in which knowledge and ideas are created and represented within disciplines. This point is illustrated by Coffin and Hewings (2003) in the following extracts from feedback on essays written by a student majoring in History and Politics on a course that also included a module on anthropology. The feedback on the left is on Paul's (not his real name) political history essay, marked by a political history tutor, the feedback on the right for an essay written for and marked by his anthropology tutor.

Paul

This is a very promising start to study of modern political history. You have argued your case well and supported it with appropriate documentary evidence . . .

Paul

You really have a problem with this essay, mainly for the reason that it is incoherent. It has no beginning, middle and end, no structure, no argument. May I suggest very strongly that you go to the study centre and make more enquiries about essay writing clinics.

(Coffin and Hewings, 2003, p45)

The feedback by the anthropology tutor does not signal disciplinary differences but rather fundamental problems with writing that result in the suggestion to seek help from the study centre. Taking Paul and Bernie's experiences together it is clear why some students can feel confused, demoralised and demotivated in their academic writing. Lea and Stierer (2000) suggest that students on practice-based courses, such as social work, face particular challenges as courses commonly include modules drawn from multiple disciplines, each with their own writing conventions. Social work courses, for example, can include modules drawn from psychology, sociology, law and social policy. These modules may be taught by subject experts from these disciplines and in some universities are delivered within different departments or even faculties. Some topics or modules within practice-based disciplines have also developed their own specific conventions. Rai (2004, 2006, Rai and Lillis, 2013) has explored the nature of academic writing in social work, in particular reflective writing for social work, as discussed in Chapter 4.

Learning the 'rules of the game', therefore, involves negotiating implicit as well as explicit writing requirements. Students need to find and negotiate formal, explicit guidelines on writing which will differ from module to module and even from assignment to assignment. Students often also encounter confusing grading and feedback from tutors which, while it might seem inconsistent, can arise from tutors conforming to disciplinary conventions that are not explained or necessarily consciously recognised by tutors.

An uneven playing field

Before you read on, review your writing on your personal language and writing histories and re-read Mark and Alisa's reflections. Despite his difficulties with spelling, Mark completed his A levels and progressed directly to university to complete a BSc before gaining social work experience and then studying for his qualifying social work masters course. He could be described as a very traditional higher education student. Alisa's experiences were very different. Despite her motivation to study and support from her family she left school at 16, demoralised by what she experienced as a lack of support at school. She worked in various jobs and began childminding when she had a son in her mid-20s. As a single parent money was tight and she decided to look into training as a social worker. She began working as an unqualified social worker, took an Access course part time and began her training in her late 30s when her son was a young teenager. Alisa's journey into higher education is typical of 'non-traditional students'.

Non-traditional students are defined by Lillis as students who have been historically excluded from higher education. These include those who are from working-class backgrounds, mature students and students from wider linguistic, cultural and religious backgrounds (2001). Lillis refers to there being an 'institutional practice of mystery' within universities which limits the participation of non-traditional students. By this she is referring to the existence of the writing conventions which underpin particular expectations of how academic knowledge is conveyed through writing which students are assumed to have acquired prior to university. Lillis refers to these ways of writing as 'conventions of literacy practice'. Put simply, students who arrive at university through a traditional route are frequently privileged in their familiarity with these conventions of writing, so many of the implicit rules of the game are already familiar, whereas non-traditional students may need to work harder to learn them. Lillis suggests that non-traditional students may have fewer opportunities to become familiar with the conventions of academic writing that students who access to higher education through more conventional routes gain over time. The gradual, incremental familiarisation with writing skills gained though systematic progression through the educational system, she suggests, advantages traditional students when they enter higher education (Lillis, 2001).

Social work has historically recruited significant numbers of students who could be described as non-traditional but over the past decade there has been an increase in fast track post graduate programmes (Hamilton, 2018). There are potential challenges in academic writing on social work programmes for both non-traditional students, as illustrated above, but also graduates from disciplines that are not closely aligned to social work. As discussed, academic writing conventions can be significantly different in particular disciplines. It can be particularly confusing for an experienced student who has performed successfully within one discipline to receive poor grades and critical feedback when writing assignments in a different discipline.

Case study

Rai (2006) reported the experiences of graduate social work students who identified the need to change the way they were accustomed to writing on previous higher education programmes studying different disciplines. One second year student participant, referred to as David, found some modules were more consistent with his previous studies, while the more practice orientated modules were very different:

(Continued)

(Continued)

> *...the challenge has been I suppose not writing an academic essay ... in [theory module] you would be unlikely to use the first person, I think that is basically the requirement to put the 'I' centre stage in [practice module]. I find it a little irritating ... I feel that it is sufficient to demonstrate your understanding and not have to, well ... the comments on the essay when you see it was that I was stand-offish. Um, I probably was but then again that's the way that I have been trained. (Student 'David')*

Rai (2006: 792)

Here David is identifying a need to reflect and write in a more personal way than is expected in many disciplines. This can be challenging for experienced academic writers as it breaks some of the rules of academic writing commonly enshrined in disciplines which do not involve an application to practise. Reflective writing, for example, is commonly included in practice-based programmes such as social work. It has particular literacy conventions which can be unfamiliar to students transferring in from, for example, other social sciences such as sociology, psychology or social policy. Reflective writing will be discussed in detail in Chapter 4.

Comment

The experiences of individual students as they embark on writing on a social work programme, therefore, will vary. There are pitfalls for both very inexperienced academic writers but also for the confident writer encountering unexpected new and contradictory conventions. Students may also discover that they find writing for some modules easier than for others. Students who are comfortable reflecting and writing about their own practice may find reflective writing much easier than students who have learnt to keep a degree of distance and objectivity (Rai, 2006).

Academic writing in the discipline of social work

As social work has developed into a discrete academic subject over the past sixty years or so, it has woven together a number of distinct disciplines together with practice learning. These individual disciplines, such as sociology, social policy and psychology, have their own established conventions around how to construct knowledge and present this in writing. This means that social work students can encounter differing expectations of their writing on individual modules or assignments, and these differences may be particularly significant where modules are taught within other departments or schools (Lyons, 1999; Baynham, 2000; Rai, 2014). While differences in writing conventions across modules is not uncommon, as we saw above with Paul's experiences in his politics and anthropology modules, it is a particularly strong feature of professional programmes such as social work and nursing:

> *So pity the poor nursing student, who is required to write at times like a sociologist, at others like a philosopher, yet again like a scientist and finally as a reflective practitioner.*

(Baynham, 2000: 17)

The way in which social work curriculum is delivered and assessed varies considerably from university to university depending on the organisational structure of the faculties, schools and departments, as you can see in the following activity.

Activity 1.5   Where is social work taught in universities?

Try searching for 'social work' across a few university websites and make a note of the school or faculty that social work is taught in at each university. How many differences are there between universities?

Comment

Doing this search at the time of writing I found social work sited in the Department of Sociology at the University of Durham, the Department of Health Professions at Plymouth University, the School of Social Sciences at Cardiff University and the School of Policy Studies at Bristol University. The departmental structure is important as it will determine whether all modules are taught within a bespoke social work curriculum area or whether some modules will be taught and assessed by lecturers in separate curriculum areas and possibly alongside students studying for different qualifications, such as sociology or psychology. The implication for writing when social work students are studying and being assessed across a range of disciplines is that they are more likely to encounter inconsistency in the expectations of their writing. This inconsistency can arise from where social work is located within the departmental structure and from the disciplinary specialisms of the lecturers setting and marking assessments. The degree of consistency will vary between universities, but even where all of the teaching is located within one department students can experience inconsistency between assessors.

While disciplinary variation can be confusing in social work writing, the centrality of practice-focused and reflective writing poses another challenge for many students. Social work programmes aim to teach students how to apply the abstract theory to practice situations. So, for example, students might learn about John Bowlby's theory of attachment (Bowlby, 1982), perhaps in a psychology module, but they would also need to demonstrate the application of this theory to their ability to understand, assesses and respond to issues of human development and parental bonding in their practice. Teaching students how to effectively apply theory to practice has posed a long-standing challenge for educators (Musson, 2017) and writing about theory in this context can also be difficult. Social work writing also frequently involves personal reflection as well as reflection on practice. The demands of reflective and practice-based writing can be considerable and will be explored in some detail in Chapter 4. Two issues that are worth briefly noting here, however, are the way in which reflective writing creates structural challenges and can potentially have an emotive impact.

Structural challenges

Much academic writing aims to be objective with the author being relatively invisible (Lillis and Rai, 2011) and one way in which this is achieved is through the avoidance of the first person, for example 'In this essay I will . . .' When writing directly about reflections on practice, personal experience or professional development it can become clumsy to avoid using the first person, so, for example, 'The author reflected on working with Mrs X' (third person) or 'Work undertaken with Mrs X was reflected on' (passive voice). It is also somewhat artificial and contrived to imply this kind of academic distance between the author and the subject matter and for this reason there is more acceptance of the use of the first person in many social work assignments. The tenses used in reflective or practice-based writing can also be tricky as the writer will often need to appropriately use the past tense (to refer to events that have happened), present tense (to reflect on these events) and future tense to discuss future planned action (Bottomley et al., 2018). This contrasts with much academic writing, where there is an expectation that the same tense is generally used throughout.

Emotional challenges

Writing about social work practice and personal reflections frequently takes students into emotionally sensitive territory that is not common in academic writing (Lillis and Rai, 2011). Writing about emotionally sensitive experiences within a genre of writing where the author is traditionally objective can create a real tension for students. This tension is even greater because the writing is being assessed so both the feedback and grade are commonly based on a wide range of outcomes unrelated to the intrinsically emotive focus. Writing about emotive topics, such as abuse, mental illness and death is difficult enough, but when the writing is being assessed on outcomes such as correct use of language, structure, references and formulating an academic argument there is the potential for feedback to be emotionally sensitised.

Introducing CAPS

So far we have considered a number of reasons for why learning to write at university can be difficult, and why writing in social work might be particularly challenging. Throughout this book we will consider many different kinds of written text commonly used in both university and social work practice. CAPS is a mnemonic which is short for Context, Audience, Purpose and Self and provides writers with a tool to use with any written task. It is particularly helpful when you encounter an unfamiliar text. The CAPS model will be applied throughout this book and will apply equally to writing tasks that are not covered here.

Context

All texts are written in a particular context and that context will have many implications for how it should be written. The two broad 'contexts' that have been discussed so far are university and practice. Both have complex organisational purposes, structures and cultures that have an impact on the conventions surrounding how students and practitioners are expected to write. These contexts will be explored in more detail throughout this book, but there are many other contexts in which writing takes place, such as creative writing, writing in business contexts and writing for social media. You may not be consciously aware these contexts exist or that they have any influence over how you write but texts produced within institutional contexts, such as universities, in particular are influenced by some powerful norms and expectations. The academic writing conventions introduced in this chapter represent some of these norms and expectations within the context of universities.

As discussed above, it would be simplistic to assume that 'university' is one, homogeneous context. Universities are complex organisations with significant variation across institutions, faculties and disciplines. There are, however, some commonalities – for example, much of the writing within universities is broadly 'academic' and written either by students as part of their assessment or by academics as part of their role as researchers and teachers. Whether writing as a student or academic, there are both explicit and implicit 'rules' which govern how texts should be written which will have an impact on how effective or successful texts are considered to be. Writing in practice has similarly complex rules and expectations which are also frequently implicit.

Practice writing across social work contexts also shares some important characteristics but just as academic conventions vary across universities, disciplines and faculties, practice writing differs across localities, agencies and service user group. This can be difficult for student social workers who often gain experience of writing in one practice context during their placement and then move on to employment in a different agency or service user group where they find the expectations of how they should write are different. Experienced practitioners can encounter the same challenges which can be perhaps even more difficult where they have become skilled and confident writing in one practice context and then need to make adjustments to meet the expectations of their new team. This is not to suggest that there are no commonalities but there can be a lack of explicit guidance which means that practitioners who move between agencies or service user groups need to do some re-learning.

Context, therefore, is multi-layered and complex. Figure 1.1 captures some of this complexity in practice and academic writing contexts.

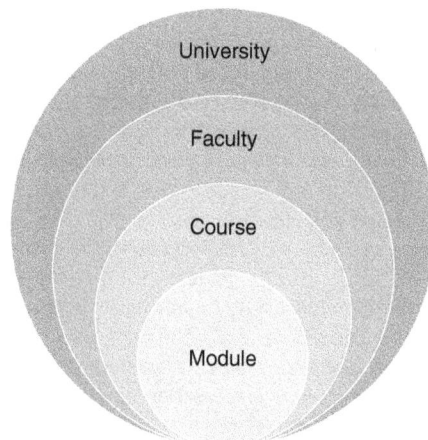

Figure 1.1 The university context

Figure 1.1 illustrates the contexts which impact on the academic writing within one university. There will be commonalities at all levels within different university faculties but there are also important differences. Figure 1.2 provides a similar illustration for practice writing.

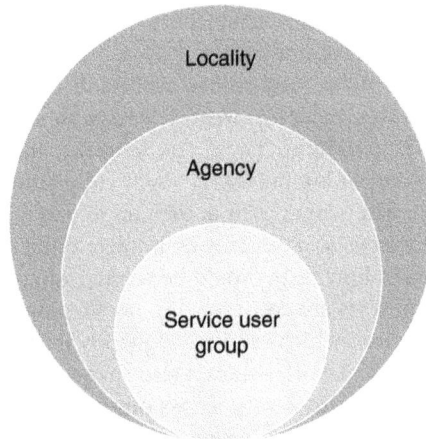

Figure 1.2   The practice context

As with the university context, there will be commonalities across all practice writing and also some within the agency, but there will be specific requirements which may differ across all of these levels.

Case Study

As a practitioner I worked in two different children and families services and then moved to an adult services team. All of these posts were within one agency, but there were significant differences between each context. My first role was within a child protection team, as it was called then, in a statutory social services team in England. I then moved to a family centre, which was jointly resourced and managed by social services and the education department. Finally I worked in a team that at the time was responsible for relocating long-term residents of hospitals for people with learning disabilities into the community. All of these teams had statutory responsibilities and there were common duties relating to data protection and access to files. Differences arose from the nature of the texts that were required and also the other agencies that each team was working closely with. The family centre included social workers and teachers, each with different roles but frequently working closely alongside each other, for example running therapeutic groups. In addition to the statutory functions of writing, such as recording and contributing to child protection assessments, the team undertook therapeutic writing alongside service users and also kept notes to facilitate planning, review and assessments within the team. The social work and teacher members of the team also had some specific requirements arising from the service that they reported to, i.e. social services or education. The community learning disability team was also multi-disciplinary and included health service members, such as occupational therapists, community nurses and consultants. As with the family centre there were some requirements shared with statutory social work colleagues but others that aligned to the requirements of the multi-disciplinary team. In both teams there were also some expectations that related to the specific communication needs of the service user groups concerned.

Comment

Understanding the context is something you will learn as you become familiar with working in a particular role or team. Effective writing will have much in common with practice in a particular context but there may also be legislation or policy guidance that you will need to identify and familiarise yourself with.

Audience

The audience for your writing is the person who you are writing it for or who you intend to read it. For personal correspondence, such as emails or SMS texts, this is normally quite straightforward as the message is addressed to one or a selected number of specific recipients. Think for a moment about the audience for a novel or a newspaper article – both novelists and journalists are writing for many people who they are unlikely to meet, so how do you think that they adjust their writing for a specific audience? Both journalists and novelists need to think about a range of features such as age and level of education. Novelists might also make assumptions about the particular interests of their audience while for many journalists it is important to consider the politics or values presumed to be common in the target audience. The audience for a student assignment is very tricky. Some students will know who is marking their assignment and they might try and write in a way which they believe the marker will approve of and therefore reward with good marks. Many universities use anonymous marking or multiple markers so that the student does not know the individual they are writing for. Both scenarios can be problematic, and the significance of audience for assessed academic writing will be considered in more detail throughout Part One of this book.

Activity 1.6   Audiences

Have a look at the following list of potential audiences. What issues might you need to think about for each of them?

- 10-year-old looked-after child
- Colleague from education
- Family carer
- Line manager
- Prospective foster carers

(Continued)

(Continued)

- Magistrate
- Adult with a learning disability
- GP

The audience in practice writing is also complex, but for different reasons. Many social work texts have multiple audiences and it is not always clear at the time of writing who these may be in the future. The nature of these audiences varies considerably too; for example, an assessment report might be intended to inform a judge, fellow professionals, parents and a child. The demands and some techniques for addressing multiple audiences are considered in Part Two.

Comment

The issues you would consider when writing for each of these audiences are very similar to those you would consider for communicating in any other way, for example taking into consideration the level of understanding and the implications of this on the vocabulary you use. Writing has an additional layer of complexity in that it can be read by different audiences and these are not always predictable at the time of writing. This might have an impact on not only what information is included in a text but also how this information is presented. One example of an agency responding to the challenge of audiences with different needs is the Islington Independent Reviewing Officer team, who review the needs of looked-after children and have developed an approach to report writing which addresses the child rather than adults the who will also read the report. This is an interesting approach which is considered in more detail in Chapter 8. Decisions about who the primary audience is are influenced by the purpose of the text.

Purpose

It might sound simple to ask what the purpose of a text is but it is very important to think carefully about why you are writing a particular text and what is it intended to achieve. In the practice context written texts have many purposes including institutional accountability, informing decision-making and maintaining records of decisions. Some texts have a statutory function, some are – at least in part – therapeutic and most are integral aspects of social work practice. It can be all too easy, however, to undertake a particular written task because it is procedurally required without thinking too much about the purpose and intended outcomes of writing it.

Activity 1.7   The purpose of assessment

Think for a moment about how you would describe the purpose of an academic assignment. Try to think of a specific assignment that you are familiar with. Why do you think this particular assignment has been designed as it has? What should be demonstrated by writing it? Do you think that it has the same purpose for the student as for the assessor?

Comment

In broad terms the purpose of academic assignments in social work is to assess the ability of the student to demonstrate competence in order to gain credit and, ultimately, professional recognition. This high-level purpose is unlikely to help students write a specific assignment effectively, so it is important to drill down to a deeper level of purpose, for example by examining the learning outcomes underpinning the assignment. Every academic assignment will provide students with a description of the task and the learning outcomes or assessment criteria that the writing will be assessed against. This information should help students to provide what the assessor is looking for and what will gain them the marks needed to pass and gain better grades. The reality of assessment is more complex than this and will be discussed in detail throughout Part One, but this formal guidance is an important starting place. Writing assignments is not only about passing and gaining credit, it is also about learning. Some assignments will not contribute to gaining credit and may not be graded – these are called 'formative' assignments as opposed to 'summative' assignments which are assessed and graded. The purposes of a formative assignment include providing an opportunity for practising and gaining feedback without the risks involved in summative assessment.

Activity 1.8   Your assignment guidance

If you have access to the assignment guidance for a course have a look at each assignment and try to find the following elements:

1.   A description of the task
2.   Learning outcomes
3.   Aims
4.   Assessment or grading criteria

Comment

How easy was it to find this information? Did all of the assignments contain the same elements and were they easy to understand? Do you think that you would understand what the purpose of the assignment was based on this guidance?

Whatever the format of the guidance, courses should provide a clear explanation of the task and how it will be assessed. Students should be clear about whether the assessment is formative or summative and the elements that they will be assessed on. The complexity arises as some elements of academic writing are not explicitly articulated, as discussed above. This is not necessarily a result of a lack of care by the staff writing the guidance, but the subtle assumptions that are made about what constitutes 'good writing' or the network of guidance that sits in different places.

Self

The final domain to consider is you, the writer. Your identity as a writer will be a theme that will run through this book and is closely associated with encouraging you to think about writing primarily as a form of communication.

Research Summary

Research on writer identity, drawing on the work of Goffman (1956), suggests that just as we play roles in different social interactions, we play roles in our writing too (Ivanič 1998). Ivanič suggests that writers can at different times present different aspects of their identity in their writing which she refers to as the 'autobiographical' self, the 'discoursal' self and the 'authorial' self. The autobiographical self draws on the writer's personal history, values and beliefs. The activities at the beginning of this chapter reflect some aspects of the autobiographical self but it can include anything about who you are as an individual and all of the past and present experiences that contribute to who you are as a person and as a writer. Identity is a complex concept but one that is important both in social work and when thinking about writing. One important aspect is that identity is not single, uniform or static. Our identities change and shift over time and encompass the many facets of who we are. Not all of these identities, or aspects of our identity, are of equal significance at all times or in all contexts. Bruner (1957) proposed the concept of 'salience' to describe the ways in which identities come to prominence in particular circumstances, with some remaining to the fore most of the time. An example would be that my identity as a woman is persistently salient, while my identity as a dog lover or an academic researcher only become salient in particular contexts and encounters. While the autobiographical self in writing potentially encompasses all of our experience, some aspects of our identity and experience will be salient, or significant, in a particular context. The autobiographical self will change over time but will not differ significantly from text to text, unlike the 'discoursal self' and 'self as author'. Ivanič suggests that the writer's knowledge, values and engagement with the context of the text are reflected through their discoursal self, sometimes unconsciously. The self as author relates to the conscious creation of an argument or representation of beliefs by the author. Ivanič suggests that the self as author is achieved when the writer gains a level of expertise and confidence in their writing and articulation of the subject.

I will illustrate the way in which all three selves can play out in a text in the context of a newly qualified social worker I will call Mark writing an assessment report in professional practice.

Case Study

Mark's autobiographical self potentially includes everything about his identity and past experiences, but of particular relevance will be how he sees himself as a writer and the personal values and beliefs he holds. Mark's autobiographical self will be an influence on everything he writes although it may change and develop over time. Mark's discoursal self reflects his professional knowledge and values applied to, in this example, an assessment report. There could be contradictions between Mark's autobiographical self and his professional role, for example Mark's political views, values or personal experience may result in a desire to provide a service in a way which is not possible within the constraints of the agency that he works for, perhaps due to budget restrictions for example. As a newly qualified worker Mark may not yet have developed an authorial self, particularly with a complex text like an assessment report. He may still be learning the nuances of writing an effective report within this context and confidently using his knowledge, values and ability to analyse complex information to present a professional judgement.

Don't worry if the concepts of autobiographical, discoursal and authorial selves seem a little confusing just now, they will be revisited throughout this book. Reflection on 'Self' for the purposes of thinking about CAPS involves reflecting on who am I writing as in this particular text. Often you may be writing from more than one position, and this applies to both academic and professional texts. As I write this I am writing as someone who used to practise as a social worker, a social work educator, a researcher, an author but also as someone who is on the same learning journey as you, trying to communicate ideas as effectively as I can.

Using CAPS to understand the demands of a new text

The reason that this book encourages writers to use CAPS as a tool for writing is that there are so many different text types which in turn vary from context to context. Writing an 'essay' is not the same on all courses in all universities: writing an assessment report for one agency in the context of mental health services will differ from a looked-after child assessment in the same agency but also from a mental health assessment in a different agency. There are of course some common threads in effective writing in both academic and professional contexts, but it would be misleading to suggest that it was possible to teach how to write a good essay or an effective assessment report in all contexts. Such a generic approach also leaves out the two most important players in written communication, the writer and the reader.

As you gain experience and confidence as a writer CAPS will become unconscious, and you will gain familiarity and confidence in your writing applied to a wider diversity of texts. CAPS is a tool to help less experienced writers, or writers encountering unfamiliar text types, to reflect on how to construct a piece of writing that will be as effective as possible for a particular context, purpose and audience. The following activity provides a step-by-step framework for using CAPS in both the academic and practice context.

Activity 1.9

Using CAPS in the academic context

1. **Context questions**

   (a) What is the question or brief? What are you being asked to do?

   (b) What are the learning outcomes or assessment criteria? Is there a marking grid or other guidance on what marks are given for and what might be penalised?

   (c) Is there general guidance at course, faculty or university level on how to write this particular kind of assignment, for example on referencing/academic conduct/plagiarism, formatting and layout or submission procedures?

   (d) Is there specific guidance for this assignment such as on word length, sources of evidence or reflections to include layout or the use of the first person?

2. **Audience questions**

   (a) Who will be marking your work? Have they marked and given feedback on pervious assessments and do you know what they expect from your writing?

   (b) Will the assignment be double marked? Do you know how this works and what the purpose is?

   (c) Do you understand who your marker expects you to think of when you write your assignment? What assumptions can you make about the reader's understanding of the subject?

3. **Purpose questions**

   (a) Is the assignment summative or formative, in other words does it contribute towards your final mark or is it for the purpose of feedback and learning only?

   (b) How does this assignment contribute to your assessment on the course overall and why are you being asked to write it?

   (c) What knowledge, skills, values or reflections does this assignment require you to demonstrate?

   (d) What mark do you need to get to pass or progress with your course?

   (e) What do you personally want to achieve with this assignment?

4. **Self-questions**

   (a) How do you feel about your writing at the moment and this particular assignment? How confident are you and do you have any particular concerns? Is there anything that worries you and do you know what you can do about any concerns?

   (b) What have you learnt from previous assignments, either writing them or the feedback you received?

   (c) What knowledge, values, skills or experiences can you draw on to write this assignment?

   (d) What support do you have available to help you write?

Using CAPS in the practice context

1. **Context questions**

   (a) Is there any guidance on writing this particular text type? Are there any local or national policies you should refer to?

   (b) Do you need to draw on or refer to any legislation?

     (c)   Does the agency you work for have any generic guidance on writing?
     (d)   Does anyone need to sign off or approve your document?
     (e)   Should other people contribute to writing the document?
     (f)   Do you need to write the document using a digital system or template?

2.   **Audience questions**

     (a)   Who are you writing the document for?
     (b)   Will it be read by more than one person?
     (c)   What should you take into account in terms of making sure the document is accessible to everyone who needs to read it?
     (d)   Are there specific issues of confidentiality you need to be aware of in terms of who will read all or part of the document?

3.   **Purpose questions**

     (a)   What do you want or need to achieve with this document?
     (b)   What outcomes do you anticipate or plan to come from writing the document?
     (c)   How will the document be used, now and potentially in the future?
     (d)   Do you need to draw on or make links to other documents?

4.   **Self-questions**

     (a)   How do you feel about your writing at the moment and this particular document? How confident are you and do you have any particular concerns? Is there anything that worries you and do you know what you can do about any concerns?
     (b)   What have you learnt from previous similar texts, either writing them or the feedback you received?
     (c)   What knowledge, values, skills or experiences can you draw on to write this document?
     (d)   What support do you have available to help you write and give you feedback?

These questions are not exhaustive and some may be irrelevant to a particular writing task, but they give you a starting point to reflect on how to plan and get started. You may want to use this as no more than a mental checklist, but you might find it helpful with some texts to use the questions as a reflective activity to help you plan your writing. If you keep a note of your planning, this can provide a useful resource to refer back to next time you write a similar text. As you read on CAPS will be considered in more detail in relation to specific kinds of writing in both the academic and practice contexts.

Chapter summary

In this chapter we have introduced the approach to writing that will be revisited throughout this book. You have reflected on who you are as a writer and how this might impact on your writings. We have explored how implicit and explicit expectations and guidance on academic writing and how to respond to the criteria which sets how your writing is judged. You have also been introduced to CAPS and the theory which underpins this approach to writing. You will return to CAPS in each chapter and explore how this can be applied to help you adapt your writing to different purposes and contexts.

Further reading

Coffin, C and Hewings, A (2003) Writing for different disciplines. In C. Coffin, M. Curry, S Goodman, A Hewings, TM Lillis and J Swann, *Teaching Academic Writing: A Toolkit for Higher Education*. London: Routledge.

This reading is useful if you would like to understand more about writing in different academic disciplines. If you are interested in reading further on writing at university outside of social work this book as a whole gives a good introduction but is a little more challenging than Crème and Lea (2008).

Crème, P and Lea, M (2008) *Writing at University: A Guide for Students*. Open University Press.

This is an excellent introductory book aimed at undergraduate students and provides guidance on writing at university.

Rai, L (2020) Writing skills for social workers. In J. Parker (ed.) *Introducing Social Work*. London: Sage.

This chapter gives an overview of the approach introduced in this chapter and goes into a little more detail about the research that underpins it.

Part One

Academic and assessed writing

2

Before you write

Introduction

In this chapter you will focus on writing for assessment during your social work course. You will think about the purpose of written assessments and reflect on some of the different kinds of written assessment and how these change the ways in which you are expected to write. Using the guidance given on academic assessments can be tricky, and you will hear from 'Suzanne' and 'Patricia' talking about their experiences of writing academic essays about practice. You will learn some strategies for understanding the guidance given to you and how this can help you plan your assignments before you begin to write.

What is the purpose of assessment?

Assessment can be a source of great anxiety for students and an unhelpful driver for learning. Many students, mature students in particular, are juggling employment and often caring commitments alongside their studies and as a result need to plan their time very carefully. This can result in a strategic approach to studying which is focused primarily on meeting the requirements of assessments rather than a more holistic approach to learning. On qualifying professional courses such as social work it is also important that teaching and assessment tasks address all of the professional requirements, and this can result in a heavy assessment load with both academic and practice assignments.

From the perspective of educators on social work programmes, assessment has a number of functions:

1. Ensuring that the required areas of learning have been studied and understood.
2. Judging the level of knowledge and academic skills achieved measured against specified requirements.
3. Judging the level of practice competence achieved measured against specified requirements.
4. As a tool to provide feedback in order to improve future learning.
5. Enabling the student to practise and develop their scholarship.
6. Enabling the student to practise and develop their practice skills.

Ensuring that the required areas of learning have been studied and understood

Every programme of study (in other words courses making up a qualification) in higher education has a curriculum which is based on specific learning that the students must study in order to successfully complete the course. Assessment tasks are based on a strategy, or plan, intended to ensure that students can demonstrate that they have acquired the required learning. The curriculum and assessment strategy are based on guidance from a number of sources, some defined by national organisations such as the Quality Assurance Agency, some set across all courses within a university and some specific to a particular programme of study. These requirements are discussed in more detail below, but they form the basis for planning an assessment strategy in order to ensure that students who pass a course have studied and understood the required content.

Judging the level of knowledge and academic skills achieved measured against specified requirements

Assessment strategies are designed to judge not only whether the required areas have been studied, but also the level of 'attainment' gained. Attainment refers to the level of success demonstrated in relation to the use and application of knowledge but also of skills, which include both practice and academic skills. Assessment strategies will not only identify what is assessed but also the way in which assessment tasks are graded. This guidance is available to students and tutors marking their work and should ensure that all students are graded fairly against the same criteria.

Judging the level of practice competence achieved measured against specified requirements

On practice courses, such as social work, students are also assessed on their practice competence through their placements. As with academic assessment there are criteria which need to be met in order to pass, but practice assessment is generally a 'threshold' assessment. This means that it is not graded but students are required to achieve a pass in order to pass the course.

As a tool to provide feedback in order to improve future learning

While not all assessment tasks contribute towards the final grade, one of the purposes of all assessment tasks is to provide students with feedback in order to help their learning. Assessments which do not count towards the final outcome of a course are called 'formative', those which do count are called 'summative'. Marking for both summative and formative assignment tasks should include feedback on what was done well, areas for improvement and, for summative work, the justification for the grade given. While it is tempting to focus only on the grade, the feedback on assignments is very important learning.

Enabling the student to practise and develop their scholarship

An important outcome of studying is developing 'scholarship' or in other words the ability to study at an advanced level. Learning how to learn, or 'metacognition', has been an important element of higher education with its roots in Ancient Greece. Mellanby and Theobald suggest that in the context of higher education: *There is a shift in gears from accumulation of information to a focus on critical thinking, reflective practice, problem-solving, and the ability to see links between disparate subjects or to relate a narrow field of study to broader perspectives* (2014, p175). Metacognition has developed a particular significance in practice subjects such as social work through the concepts of 'reflective practice' and 'reflective learning' developed by Kolb (1970), Schön (1989) and Eraut (1994). Academic writing, which also draws on the ability to research, read, comprehend, synthesise and use information critically to construct reasoned arguments is a key element of scholarship.

Enabling the student to practise and develop their practice skills

Practice learning and assessment has equal weight on social work courses alongside academic scholarship. Practice requirements involve completing a prescribed number of days but also successfully completing assessment tasks intended to demonstrate competence in practice. Some of the evidence of competence is provided through the reports or testimonials of others, such as practice educators and service users. Students are also required to complete written tasks, commonly involving a portfolio of evidence to demonstrate competence.

Activity 2.1

Look at the assignments you are required to do for your course and try to answer the following questions:

1. Which of your assignments assess primarily academic learning, which ones assess your practice and which draw on learning from both?
2. How are skills (academic and practice) assessed on your course? Is there a separate grading method for these?
3. Which assignments are marked as pass/ fail and which are graded? Does the grade contribute to your final award for the course?
4. Are any of your assignments 'formative'?
5. What feedback, other than a grade, do you receive on your assignments and how are you encouraged to use this?

Comment

You may not have found it easy to access the answers to these questions as assessment guidance can be complex and provided in different places in your course and university documentation. If you are not sure about what is assessed and how you should seek advice from your tutors. Most courses will have a process for assessing both practice and academic skills. As discussed above, practice assessments are normally a pass/fail 'threshold' while academic skills are normally assessed as an element of your summative written academic assignments. Whether an assignment is formative or summative it is important to gather as much learning and advice as possible from the feedback, although there is a temptation to focus more on the grade only. The feedback given should be valuable learning about your writing which gives you guidance on how to improve your work for the following assignments.

What requirements are students assessed against?

Social work programmes are designed around academic and professional standards that students need to meet in order to pass both the academic and professional requirements for the level of study at university and for the body which sets the standards for the profession. The details of these standards and even the body responsible for them can change over time and are also based on the nation in which you are studying and working. This dual academic and professional approach to standards is common across most professional qualifying courses in higher education. At the time of writing the standards for social work in the UK are based on requirements from the bodies discussed below.

The Quality Assurance Agency

The Quality Assurance Agency (QAA) sets 'subject benchmarks' for a range of disciplines including social work and these are reviewed and updated periodically. They were last published in 2016, but the most recent versions are available online. The current benchmark standards detail subject knowledge and understanding includes:

- Social work theory
- Values and ethics
- Service users and carers
- The nature of social work
- Leadership, organisation and delivery.

In addition to the benchmark details the required skills are as follows:

- Problem-solving skills
- Communication skills
- Skills in working with others
- Skills in personal and professional development
- Use of technology and numerical skills.

(QAA, 2019)

In addition to the subject benchmarks, which are specific to social work, the QAA publishes guidance on standards which are generic to all higher education courses which are intended to ensure common standards of quality across all universities (QAA, 2013).

The professional standards for social work

The professional standards for social work are governed locally within each nation. At the time of writing responsibility for professional standards in England is transferring from the Health Care Professions Council to Social Work England. In addition the British Association of Social Work (BASW) produced a Professional Capabilities Framework (PCF) which sets out standards for professional development from point of entry to training up to the highest level, which is 'strategic social worker' and applies to England. The PCF was refreshed in 2018 (BASW, 2018). In Wales the code of conduct is set by Social Care Wales. In Scotland the Standards in Social Work Education (SiSWE) bring together the QAA subject benchmark and generic standards alongside the Scottish professional standards so that all guidance is in one document, The Framework for Social Work Education in Scotland (SSSC, 2003). In Scotland there are also further standards specific to mental health, childhood practice and residential childcare. In Northern Ireland the standards are set by the Northern Ireland Social Care Council (NISCC). You can read the detailed guidance for each nation through the following links:

- Social Work England: https://socialworkengland.org.uk/
- BASW PCF: https://www.basw.co.uk/professional-development/professional-capabilities-framework-pcf
- SiSWE: https://www.gov.scot/publications/framework-social-work-education-scotland/pages/5/
- SSSC: https://www.sssc.uk.com/the-scottish-social-services-council/

Although the detail of the professional standards and the agencies responsible for them differs across the nations of the UK, all share an adherence to the QAA standards and have National Occupational Standards (NOS) which govern professional practice pre- and post-qualifying. There is much commonality across the four nations, but universities are still required to ensure that training and assessment meets the requirements for the nation in which they are based. National universities, such as the Open University, meet the standards for all of the nations.

You will spend a considerable amount of time writing during your university studies, on your practice placement and in practice post-qualification. Recent research suggests that social workers spend at least 50 per cent of their time writing (Lillis et al., 2017) and although you may be assessed through a variety of methods, these will primarily be written forms of communication. Despite the significance of writing in academic and practice contexts, there is relatively little mention of it in the standards governing education or training in social work. There are references to writing requirements in both the QAA and the national occupational standards and these are in the context of:

- communication (through writing for different audiences, purposes and contexts)
- case recording
- report writing.

The QAA qualifications framework does not make explicit reference to writing but does refer to the general application of skills to learning and assessment.

The absence of detailed requirements or universal guidance means that the standards and expectations of writing during qualifying training is set by the universities which deliver social work programmes. In common with other academic disciplines this means that there are considerable differences between programmes. Research into student writing (for example, Crème and Lea, 2008; Lillis, 2001; Lillis and Turner, 2001; Lea and Stierer, 2000) has shown that students need to negotiate and interpret a complex set of implicit rules which govern how their writing is assessed, and this applies equally to social work.

Cracking the code

Activity 2.2

For this activity you need to find the assessment criteria for one of the assignments on your course. You may find that there is specific guidance for each task and also some generic guidance that applies to all of your assessments, so you will need to look at both of these. Looking at all of the guidance, along with any feedback you have received on assignments you have already completed, fill in Table 2.1.

Comment

The topics in Table 2.1 are commonly included in assignment guidance and marking criteria, but you may find that not all appear in your own guidance. The importance attached to each topic may be very different and it is also common for the ways in which each topic is interpreted or defined to differ within each programme and even between modules or units. As discussed in Chapter 1, there are significant differences between the expectations of academic writing in different disciplines but also that requirements are interpreted differently by different tutors and so it is important to seek as much clarity as possible before you write. Don't assume that the expectations across modules/units – or indeed between tutors – will be the same. It is advisable to take up any opportunities offered by your course to discuss the ways in which assignments will be marked, ideally with tutor who will be marking. Remember that staff in libraries and study support centres will frequently support students from across many courses and so may not have as detailed an understanding of the specific requirements of your course as your subject specialist tutors.

Table 2.1 What are the requirements given to you in the following areas?

Topic	No guidance	Details of guidance given
Use of English/correct grammar, punctuation, etc.		
Structure and/or organisation of the assignment		
Referencing/academic practice		
Use of practice/application to practise		
Use of reflection		
Use of literature/theory/reading		
Analysis/critical analysis/development of an argument		
Addressing anti-discriminatory practice/inequality/oppression, etc.		
Use of values and/or ethics		
Relevant content/use of knowledge		
Style		
Other		

Learning outcomes

It is very common for guidance on modules or courses to include 'learning outcomes', or in other words a summary of the learning that a student must or should achieve after completing a particular unit of study. Learning outcomes can be used at the level of the whole programme of study but also for specific modules or units within them.

They normally provide a guide to the teaching that will be delivered and also the criteria that students will be assessed against. Advance HE, the national organisation which provides guidance to universities, suggests that learning outcomes should be:

- written in the future tense
- identify important learning requirements
- be achievable and assessable
- use clear language easily understandable to students.

(Advance HE, 2010)

Learning outcomes are very important when completing your assignments as they are the way in which markers will judge your writing. They should provide consistency across a cohort of students as they are applied to all students. When planning an assignment you are likely to be given a title or a task description which should guide your planning, but it will be the learning outcomes that are used to assess your work. Whenever you begin a new module or unit make sure that you find the learning outcomes and check which learning outcomes will be assessed in each assignment. Where there is more than one assignment task not all of the learning outcomes will be assessed in each, so it is important to be clear about which learning outcomes apply to each task.

Activity 2.3

1. Look at the guidance on a module/unit that you are studying and find the learning outcomes.

    (a) Are there also learning outcomes for the whole programme of study?

2. Within one module/unit of study read the guidance on the assignment tasks and look to see if there are learning outcomes for the assignment.

    (a) Are all of the module learning outcomes assessed in each task or are they distributed across the tasks?
    (b) Do you think that they meet the Advance HE criteria outlined above?

In some universities the terminology used for learning outcomes may be slightly different so if you are unable to find any references to learning outcomes it is worth asking for advice from your tutor.

Preparing to write

This book is about writing, but in education writing is primarily a tool to capture your thinking and demonstrate your learning. It is of course important that your writing is clear and can be understood through the use of correct grammar, spelling and punctuation but the focus here is on what you write rather than just how you write. Assessments are set in order for you to:

- demonstrate that you have gained and understood the knowledge specified in the learning outcomes
- applied or used the specified knowledge, for example to practise
- demonstrated the required skills, which may be academic, practice or both
- followed the specified requirements such as word length, referencing, structure, etc.

All of these areas will be discussed in more detail in the chapters that follow in relation to specific writing tasks, so this section is a general introduction to the preparatory tasks involved in writing an assignment. The preparatory tasks introduced here are gathering information, note-taking, thinking and planning, and evidencing your work.

Gathering information

The learning that is used to construct your writing will come from a range of sources and this will depend in part on your mode of study. Most courses will expect some learning to come from given content and content you have found for yourself. Given content refers to material from lectures, tutorials, workshops and handouts on online resources. Content that you find yourself might be in the form of books, journal articles or reflections drawn from practice. Gathering information takes time and it is important to allow sufficient time to search for relevant material, read slowly and think. Styles of studying vary, some people will prefer to read widely and then select relevant material to develop and use in an assignment while others will plan the assignment and then selectively seek out relevant reading. Others will use a combination. Increasingly reading is available online, making accessing it relatively quick, but if there are specific books or articles which are not available online then you need to allow time to access hard copies, either via your library or bookshop.

Note-taking

One of the purposes of taking notes is to identify the content that you will use in your assignment. Taking notes can help you to make sense of a large amount of information and begin to focus on the material that will be relevant for your assignment. There are many ways to take notes and finding one that works for you will be a personal decision. Some of the techniques that can be useful are:

- highlighting or underlining, either a hard copy printout or digital document
- using marginal comments
- summarising each reading with bullet points or key words
- identifying themes across a range of sources and writing notes on each, for example using a table as in Figure 2.1.

	Biological	Families	Cultures
Key researches	Mednick and others	Chicago School Shaw and McKay	Clarke and Coleman
Causes of crime	Genetic predisposition	Generational transmission of criminal careers in problem families	Zones of transition; power rule; gang sub-culture; crime not seen as normative problem.
Evidence	Twin studies Adoption studies	Longitudinal studies	Geographical surveys Participant observation
Weakness	Corporate crime? Social assumptions?	What is good parenting? Role of education, class, culture?	Cultures without gangs? Role of economics?

Figure 2.1 Tabulated notes

Source: Open University (2020). Study Skills Figure. At: https://help.open.ac.uk/tables (accessed 16 June 2020).

Thinking and planning

Thinking and planning will occur throughout your reading and note-taking phases but it is important to pause and create a plan for your assignment before you begin to write. Your plan should be based on the assignment task and learning outcomes that you need to meet and should also enable you to make a link between what you want to say and the evidence from your reading. One of the ways in which academic writing differs from writing you may do in your personal life is that you need to back-up statements that you make with evidence, generally from a published source such as a book, journal article or sometimes a website. This will be discussed in more detail throughout this book. Creating a careful plan can help you to stay focused once you begin to write, to check that you are answering the question and to help you make sure that you keep track of the evidence that you are using.

Referencing

The purpose of referencing is to acknowledge the sources of evidence that you have used in your writing. Acknowledging the work of other writers is a core element of academic conduct and there can be severe penalties for students who consistently fail to reference correctly as this is considered to be plagiarism, or the passing of someone else's work as your own. The technicalities of correct referencing can be a source of frustration and anxiety for many students, but the crucial and core principal of good academic conduct is that you should always acknowledge the use of other people's ideas and words by providing a reference. There are different styles of referencing, Harvard being one of the most common, and your university will provide detailed guidelines and examples to enable you to reference correctly.

Case Study

Suzanne

Suzanne was a second-year social work student, undertaking a placement in a hospital team. Her course involved assessment through an essay on two modules, one assessing practice and the other assessing applied social sciences. These two modules had very different requirements despite being included in the same course. Suzanne was confused about the difference between the requirements of these two essays, despite reading the guidance very carefully and talking to her tutors on each module. Suzanne identified that the social science module required a more traditional academic style, using the third person, while the practice module encouraged self-reflection on not only practice but personal experiences such as feelings. Suzanne realised through talking to her tutor that these reflections still needed to be linked to theoretical reading. It was only on the feedback after her essay for the practice module had been assessed that she understood that her tutor also expected her to reflect on how her attitudes and understanding (about privacy) had changed as a result of her practice. The written guidance, advice from her tutor and the feedback finally clarified exactly what was required for this particular assignment, which was very different from Suzanne's previous experience of academic writing, but the feedback came after her work was assessed and so was accompanied by some lost marks. The following extract is Suzanne's reflections:

> It's the style that is so different because (Practice tutor) wants 'I want, I think, I feel I felt' whereas the (social sciences tutor) is looking at writing in the third person. Well, you write that to your auntie Jane, you don't write it for a course, I've never written it for a course. The one thing he said to me when I did ring him up was that you need to make a link, I told him what I was thinking about, and I said I want to use this. And this is the experience and he said that sounds fine but you must make a clear link and I thought I'll make a link if it kills me and I did and he has written a clear link, you know it would be worth saying a little more about how you see these issues now privacy has become more important for you? And I'm thinking, well I don't know that you want to know that.

(Continued)

(Continued)

This extract illustrates the confusion that Suzanne felt arising from the differing requirements of writing style between courses and which can sometimes be attributed to the
preferences of particular tutors.

Comment

A common theme arising in discussions with students is the inconsistency of marking
between tutors. Universities go to great effort to try and standardise the ways in which
grades are given but even with very carefully crafted guidance and procedures the grading of academic work comes down to an individual interpretation of the requirements.
Universities will hold standardisation meetings for some assessments, particularly
examined/end-of-module tasks in which tutors grade samples of work independently and
then compare their grades in order to try and establish a common standard. I have always
been struck by the significant discrepancy in grading even between very experienced
tutors. This can particularly occur with assignments which are original and can be judged
as either exceptional or borderline fails. There can be 'triggers of concern' based on, for
example, poor or erratic use of correct English language or use of practice which for some
tutors can result in disproportionate concerns which overshadow assignments which
broadly meet the learning outcomes. There is also a risk that an assignment which begins
weakly, be it with poor use of language, unclear structure or a lack of sharp focus on the
topic, will not be able to 'recover' the trust of the marker even if across the whole assignment on balance the work meets the brief. While this may seem unfair to students it is
unfortunately often unconscious and results from the fact that applying marking criteria
inevitably involves individual interpretation, drawing on the individual experiences and
judgements of each tutor.

Using feedback

Suzanne's experiences illustrate the importance of using feedback alongside the guidance
on writing assignments. Some caution is needed when applying the feedback on one
module to another as the marking criteria may differ between modules. On social work
programmes, for example, it is common for students to study theoretical modules, such
as sociology or psychology alongside more practice-focused, applied modules. The theoretical modules may even be taught by non-social work lecturers and classes may include
students who are not studying social work. This means that the expectations around how
assignments are written can be very different, for example in expectations around using
the passive voice rather than the first person, which is much more acceptable in practice-
orientated modules which require reflection on practice. This is discussed in more depth
in Chapter 4.

On modules where there is more than one assignment the feedback can be invaluable as
it is more likely that the expectations can be safely applied to all assignment tasks. There is a
temptation for students to focus mainly, or entirely, on the final grade when they receive their
marked work back, and clearly the grade is important in terms of the final result for the
course. It is the feedback, however, which should help you learn from your assignment and
to improve the way in which you write and present your ideas in future assignments.

Concern is frequently expressed about whether students use the feedback provided or only look at the final grade. Jackson (2017) suggests that there are many reasons why students might not read and use feedback: it can be perceived as being irrelevant to future assignments, where a grade is good it can be considered unnecessary and where bad demoralising. Jackson (2017) identifies the emotional response of students to assignment feedback and the impact that this can have on learning. There are many reasons why students can have a strong emotional response to feedback. Firstly it can spark memories of learning as a child, this may even be subconscious but result in the impact of negative feedback in particular being very difficult to read. In social work, however, there is an added dimension as where an assignment requires you to reflect on practice or personal experiences these are often associated with very strong feelings, as illustrated by the experience of Patricia.

Case Study

Patricia

Patricia's feedback on her writing led her to believe that, despite having shared very intimate experiences and reflected on values which placed her in an emotionally vulnerable position, she had not met her tutor's expectations. In the following extended extract from Patricia's writing, she reflects on working with a dying woman and the consequent impact of this work on her own thoughts about death and bereavement:

I have worked in partnership with Ann to gain her trust and to advocate on her behalf as she has tried to assimilate so much distressing information and navigate her way through unfathomable depths of loss – loss of independence, of dignity, of credibility and ultimately of life itself. I reflect that the strength of my support for Ann is largely a result of the empathy I feel for her as she attempts to protect her values from being compromised. The positive identity, with which Ann was admitted to hospital, is being systematically undermined by the inference that she is unreasonable, unrealistic and difficult, basically because she has refused to conform. Individuals who are perceived as 'difficult' appear to find it hard to take advantage of the opportunities for choice. In this instance Ann is both being labelled and being discouraged from making an informed choice about where she feels her future care needs should be met even after her death. There have also been questions raised about Ann's competency in decision-making given the progressive nature of her illness. These are all issues with which I identify and I have during the past six weeks taken significant steps to protect both my personal privacy and my family should I ever be diagnosed with a life-limiting illness or meet an untimely death. I have made a will, identified potential guardians for my children, shared with a close friend the location of private documentation, identified a responsible person who is prepared to have Power of Attorney should it ever be necessary and I have disposed of anything incriminating! I feel that my involvement with Ann has given me a focus in terms of my own values. To help Ann to resolve some of the internal struggles she has faced in response of her impending death, it has been necessary for me to explore some of my own anxieties in terms of my own morbidity.

(Continued)

(Continued)

Tutor feedback: ✓ a clear link. It would be worth saying a little more about how you see these issues now. Has privacy become more important – it seems so, and with looking at what this meant before the case happened. Remember that looking at change implies saying where you were before the situation arose – that would be useful to comment upon in the future in relation to writing about personal development.

Comment

Working with a terminally ill woman preparing for her own death and loss of freedom and identity confronted Patricia with her own death, motivating her to take action to prepare for any unexpected incapacity. Patricia shares deeply emotive personal information about herself in this essay but despite this intimate disclosure, her tutor encourages her to disclose even more of her thoughts and feelings about her death. This example is indicative of not only the depth and extent that students are expected to share personal experiences in some essays but also the way that personal change (relating to beliefs and actions) is expected.

Patricia's case study illustrates the way in which very emotive content is routinely included in academic essays, particularly where reflection is required. Receiving feedback on essays can therefore be greatly sensitised and great care is needed to ensure that remarks are sensitive to the emotional investment that a student may have made. Feedback relating to matters such as spelling, style or structure can be experienced as insensitive or devaluing although this is not the intention of the marker. Feedback asking for further or deeper personal reflections, as Patricia experienced, can also feel intrusive and unreasonable in the context of academic work. Providing such personal reflections in assignments is uncomfortable for many people but also contradicts the conventions of academic writing in non-practice disciplines. If you have studied and become familiar with this more detached academic style it can be confusing and challenging to adapt to a more reflective style. The challenges of reflective writing are discussed in more depth in Chapter 4.

Chapter summary

In this chapter we have focused on preparing to write. We have looked at finding your way around the guidance and understanding why it is there. We have looked at some of the challenges that students experience in trying to understand and apply guidance on writing assignments. We have also explored some of the techniques that can help you get well prepared before you begin to write, such as making a plan, taking effective notes and learning from feedback from previous assignments.

Further reading

Bottomley, J, Cartney, P and Pryjmachuk, S (2018) *Studying for Your Social Work Degree* (Critical Study Skills). St Albans: Critical Publishing.

This slim book gives an accessible guide to studying in higher education and making the most of the learning experiences available. It includes discussion of how to prepare for your assignments and use feedback.

Walker, H (2011) *Studying for Your Social Work Degree*. Exeter: Learning Matters.

This is a more comprehensive book. It contains a chapter on preparing for academic study and also on writing academically in social work.

Writing an essay

Introduction

In this chapter we will consider the essay as a form of assessment and what is involved in writing successful essays. You will explore the requirements on your own course and think about how to prepare for writing an essay, including reading, taking notes and making a plan for how to structure your essay. You will also learn about the importance of building an argument in your essays, using evidence to support your arguments and what is meant by developing a scholarly voice. Finally we will reflect on why writing essays is helpful for you as a social worker and about the links to practice.

What is an essay?

The essay is perhaps the most common form of written assessment in higher education and many written assignments are referred to as 'essays' even though what is required may differ significantly. Many people will also have been introduced to essays at school and may assume that they are familiar with what writing an essay involves.

Activity 3.1

1. How would you describe an essay to someone who had to write one for the first time?
2. How is an essay different from other kinds of writing?

Write some notes for yourself and try to come up with three or four words that you think capture what an essay is.

Comment

It is likely that everyone will define the essay differently based on their own experiences. Keep hold of the notes you make as you read this chapter and once you get to the end return to them and see whether you would now change your definition at all.

Research Summary

Although most people will be familiar with the word 'essay' it can refer to very different things. Research challenges the idea that the essay is easily defined (Baynham, 2000; Lea and Street, 1998; Lea and Stierer, 2000; Lillis, 2001; Street, 1984) and suggest that the requirements vary and are based upon discipline-specific conventions, as discussed in Chapter 1. There is a risk that it is assumed that essays are 'common sense' and that students will arrive on courses sufficiently familiar with the requirements of essay writing from their previous studies so that they should be able to transfer these writing skills to higher education (Lillis, 1997). Lillis identifies particular difficulties with what she calls 'essayist literacy':

> Essayist literacy provides a way of talking about student writing which acknowledges the relationship between literacy practices and knowledge making practices whilst situating both within a specific socio-historical position.

> (Lillis 2001, p40)

Lillis indicates here that conventions around how to write an essay relate to the ways in which knowledge is conveyed as well as structural issues such as the layout, style and organisation of writing. As a result assumptions should not be made that students – or indeed tutors – share a common understanding of what is meant by the term 'essay' or what is judged to be a good essay. The disciplinary differences within social work can result in a diversity of writing conventions not only within one course but also between assignments, even where they are similarly labelled as 'essays'.

> The presumption of a generic set of academic writing conventions is problematic, even within one 'discipline', and this is compounded where one course of study includes diverse disciplines. The foundation course, as a broad theoretical course providing the knowledge underpinning care, drew upon a range of social science disciplines, including sociology, psychology and social policy.

> (Rai 2008, p236)

When you write for your social work programme you are likely to need to write essays but also many different kinds – or genres – of text. The concept of a 'genre' is a way of describing or grouping particular styles or functions of writing. In academic writing these could include, for example, essays, posters, laboratory reports, examination papers, case studies or research papers. There are a large number of academic genres which you night come across as a student, and while there are some commonalities that define a genre, within each one there can also be significant differences in what is required.

Activity 3.2

Look at the information that you have on the assessments for your own course and use this to fill in a table like the following. Add in columns so you have one for each assignment task and if none of the genre types seems to fit the description, add additional genres – or task types – at the end.

	Assignment 1	Assignment 2	Assignment 3	Assignment 4	Assignment 5	Assignment 6
Essay						
Case study						
Reflective journal						
Examination						
Multiple choice/short answer						
Dissertation						
Portfolio						
Report						
Other						

Comment

Your assignment guidance may have given you an indication of a genre in the title or instructions; however, if this was not the case you may have found it quite difficult to decide what genre each assignment task was. Even when the word 'essay' is used in the guidance you may find things unclear, for example if within an essay you are being asked to reflect, draw on a case study or report findings you have been asked to research. This lack of clarity can arise from assignment guidance being imprecisely worded, but it is also an indication of the fluid nature of genres which are in reality rarely precisely defined or delineated. You will be looking in some detail at genres other than the essay as you work through this book but as you consider the essay in some depth it is useful to be aware that there are other genres and that there can be an overlap between them.

(Continued)

(Continued)

The simplest dictionary definition of an essay is 'a short piece of writing on a particular subject' (Oxford Dictionaries, 2020) but this masks the complexity involved in understanding what is required by markers when writing an essay. In the context of this book the essay is broadly defined by the following characteristics, all discussed in more detail throughout this chapter. It is important to remember that there are no firm, clear or consistent definitions of any genre. The following characteristics should help you reflect on and plan your writing, but you should always be guided by the specific brief given to you for a specific assignment task on your course.

1. **Response to a title**
2. **Length** – an essay is normally a reasonably substantial piece of writing – at degree and master's level it is commonly between 1,000 and 8,000 words. It is common for courses to allow any academic assignment to be 10 per cent longer or shorter than the target word limit without penalty.
3. **Structure** – there is a classic or typical structure to an essay involving an introduction and conclusion at the beginning and end and a number of themed paragraphs making up the body of the essay.
4. **Focus** – in the context of an academic essay, it is normally a response to a question, proposition or statement. Examples of essay 'questions' are discussed below.
5. **Argument** – essays are normally what can be referred to as rhetorical or persuasive texts. This just means that within the essay the writer should be putting forward one of more arguments or points of view based on their analysis of evidence.
6. **Evidence** – the argument within an essay should be based on evidence, and this is commonly in the form of references to published writing such as books, journals, articles or websites, discussed further under 'Doing your research' below.
7. **Analysis** – part of the process of constructing an argument involves the writer selecting and weighing up evidence and then providing evaluative comment. This is not the same as including personal opinion, but it does involve the writer using their own judgement based on the selected evidence.

This is not a definitive list of the features of an essay, but it does capture the main elements which are commonly expected and assessed by markers in under- and post-graduate courses.

Different kinds of title

There are many ways in which an essay 'question' can be worded and some are not in fact in the form of a question. Here are a few examples of a similar essay title worded in different ways:

1. Why is inter-professional working a vital aspect of social work practice?
2. Inter-professional working is a vital aspect of social work. Discuss.
3. Write a 3,000 word essay explaining the importance of inter-professional working to social work practice.
4. Analyse the benefits and challenges of inter-professional working in social work.

All of these titles – or questions – could prompt a very similar essay. A useful technique when reading an essay title or question is to highlight the key words. All of these examples share the key words 'inter-professional working' and 'social work practice'. These key words give you the main content focus for your essay. Each question or title also includes a word which indicates what you should do:

Example 1 = Why

Example 2 = Discuss

Example 3 = Explaining

Example 4 = Analyse

Although the wording is different, each example is asking the writer to explore the importance of inter-professional working in the context of social work practice. At degree level and higher there is commonly an expectation of at least some analysis, which in the context of this title might be evaluating the benefits and challenges involved in inter-professional working. Example 4 clearly indicates that this analysis is required. The benefits and challenges of other formats are less explicit, although there may be clues about the analysis required within the detailed guidance if this has been provided. The requirement for analysis, whether specifically based on the challenges and benefits or not, may also be specified in the assignment 'rubric'. The rubric details the guidance on how scores are allocated for different elements of the assignment.

Doing your research

Once you have thought carefully about the question or title it is time to do your research, which for most essays will mean reading although some practice- or research-based essays may require you to gather data from practice or other research sources. The source for any evidence should be reliable and accurate, so for example it should be published and have been through a quality and validity process, such as peer review. A peer review is when other academics evaluate writing prior to publication to ensure that it is suitable for publication. Some sources, particularly website pages, have not been through such a process and therefore *may* contain unreliable or biased content which is a poor basis for evidence. Evidence drawn on should be correctly acknowledged through the provision of references.

The classic structure

There may be specific guidance from your course on how to structure an essay. If this is the case then you should follow the structure suggested. As discussed above a classic essay structure is based on an introduction and conclusion with several paragraphs which form the main body in between them. The reason for a clear structure is to help the reader to follow the ideas and evidence laid out in your essay. It can also help you as a writer to organise your thoughts, evidence and arguments.

Introduction

The purpose of the introduction is to tell the reader clearly and briefly what the essay will cover. It can be helpful to write your introduction after you have completed the first draft of your essay, or at least after you have written a detailed plan so that you are already clear about what your essay will contain. The introduction is very important as it is the first thing that your marker will read. If it is confusing, overly wordy or contains language errors (such as spelling or punctuation) it may influence the marker's impression of the rest of your essay. It can help to check your introduction against the essay title or question – have you used the key words? Does your introduction tell the marker how you will respond to the question or task? Have you mentioned any key theories that are included in your essay? The following introduction is just one way in which you might open an essay based on Example 4: Analyse the benefits and challenges of inter-professional working in social work.

This essay will explore the benefits and challenges of inter-professional working in social work, drawing on the example of child protection. It will outline the concerns raised in public reports about the effectiveness of inter-professional working, including the Seebohm Report 1968, the Butler-Sloss Inquiry 1988 and the Laming Report of the Victoria Climbié Inquiry 2003. The benefits of inter-professional working will be outlined in the context of current child protection practice, with reference to the principles of the Children Act 1989. The persisting challenges of collaborating across agencies will be analysed, including differing organisational cultures and methods of communication. Finally, with reference to Muller (2019) and French (2017), some strategies for enhancing the effectiveness of inter-professional working will be offered.

(**Note**: The reports and legislation referred to here are factual but the references are fictionalised.)

Taking this exemplar sentence by sentence, it is effective in the following ways:

Table 3.1   Annotated example of an introduction

This essay will explore the benefits and challenges of inter-professional working in social work, drawing on the example of child protection.	Makes reference to the key words in the title
It will outline the concerns raised in public reports about the effectiveness of inter-professional working, including the Seebohm Report 1968, the Butler-Sloss Inquiry 1988 and the Victoria Climbié Inquiry 2003: Inquiry Report.	Signals the theoretical/legislative references that will be used
The benefits of inter-professional working will be outlined in the context of current child protection practice, with reference to the principles of the Children Act 1989.	Refers to a *description* of the benefits
The persisting challenges of collaborating across agencies will be analysed, including differing organisational cultures and methods of communication.	Refers to a *critical analysis* of the challenges
Finally, with reference to Muller (2019) and French (2017), some strategies for enhancing the effectiveness of inter-professional working will be offered.	Refers to an *analytical application* of theory to practice with reference to the key words.

Main body

The main body of your essay should be made up of paragraphs which should ideally contain one discussion point which is clearly linked to the paragraph that comes before and after. This linking, sometimes referred to as 'signposting', is an effective way to help the reader to follow your discussion. Examples of useful signposting phrases are:

Building on the idea that . . .

- *When applying this idea to . . .*
- *Following on from the idea that . . .*
- *As discussed above . . .*
- *In contrast . . .*
- *In the next section/paragraph this essay will turn to . . .*

There is no rule for the length of a paragraph but in order to explain the discussion point they will generally need to be more than a couple of sentences and not so long that the reader loses focus on the point being made. Very roughly around 200–400 words is an effective length for each paragraph. Very short paragraphs can give your marker the impression your ideas are disjointed and that you have not been able to link them together into a cogent argument. Very long paragraphs result in a rambling and unfo-cused read, making it hard to follow the key ideas or overall argument. An effective plan is a very helpful tool to organise your ideas into paragraphs. This very simple plan based on the example essay question above illustrates one way to use your plan to map out your para-graphs. You may find some points are more complex and need more than one paragraph. This structure would equate roughly to a 2,500–3,000 word essay.

Table 3.2   Example of an essay plan

Paragraph number	Focus
1	Introduction
2	Defining inter-professional working
3	Concerns raised in historical inquiries
4	Continuing importance today
5	Benefits of inter-professional working: for safe social work practice
6	Benefits of inter-professional working: for service user involvement
7	Evaluate reasons for challenges: professional and agency culture, communication systems, time pressures
8	Introduce strategies drawing on Muller and French
9	Critique strategies using Muller and French
10	Conclusion

Conclusion

One helpful guide for your conclusion is that it should not contain any new information. The purpose of the conclusion is to very briefly summarise the points made in your essay. As with the introduction, the conclusion is very important as it leaves the marker with a final impression of your work. It is an opportunity for you to demonstrate that you have really understood the points that you have made through your ability to summarise them succinctly. A useful strategy for your conclusion is also to refer back to the question to reassure your marker that you have fully answered it. This is also a really good check for yourself as it is possible to write a very good essay that has drifted from the question or title in one or more important ways. For example, using the illustrated essay above, make sure that you have addressed both challenges *and* benefits, and that these have been applied to social work practice.

Taking a position: crafting an argument

One of the defining features of an academic essay is that it should construct an argument. In this context an argument refers to the process of evaluating the ideas from your research and drawing a conclusion. There are many ways in which arguments can be constructed but all will involve the writer using evidence from reading/research in order to build a case for a particular position or view – this is sometimes referred to as 'taking a position'. Constructing an argument using critical analysis is one of the most challenging aspects of academic writing and is one of the defining features of higher-level academic study. In entry-level (or pre-entry level) assessments students may be able to pass with primarily descriptive essays. As you move through the levels of study, however, there is an increasing expectation that description is replaced by more critical, evaluative and analytical writing. One way to think about this is through the following process, here illustrated with some possible arguments based on the essay title explored above: Analyse the benefits and challenges of inter-professional working in social work.

Table 3.3 Building an argument

Question	Evidence of argument for	Evidence of argument against	Author's position
Do assessments of risk depend on inter-professional practice?	Outline and explain evidence	Outline and explain evidence	Risk cannot be safely assessed without the perspectives of professionals from different agencies
Is inter-professional working overly time-consuming?	Outline and explain evidence	Outline and explain evidence	When built into training and an integral part of work
Do the benefits outweigh the challenges?	Outline and explain evidence	Outline and explain evidence	There are significant challenges which can slow down the process of assessment and make it more complex. On balance this is outweighed by the benefits as safe assessment of risk and planning rely on inter-professional input.

Many students find it very difficult to write essays which are based on argument and analysis rather than description, so don't worry if this seems a challenge. Markers are aware that moving from description to analysis is difficult and to gain a pass you will generally not be expected to maintain an analytical stance throughout the essay until higher levels of study such as the latter half of an undergraduate degree or post-graduate levels.

Activity 3.3

Read the following two paragraphs, one of which is descriptive and one of which is constructed around an analytical argument. Identify which paragraph contains an argument and then note down how you could identify it. One way to identify the more analytical paragraph is to underline or highlight the individual words which suggest that the author is making an evaluation or judgement on the evidence.

Paragraph one

Inter-professional working has been an important feature of child protection assessments since the Butler-Sloss Inquiry (1988) and was identified earlier than this in the Seebohm Report (1968). The Butler-Sloss Inquiry was significant as it raised the profile of inter-professional working and the risks posed by practitioners from different professions failing to share information effectively. There was particular concern about medical practitioners sharing information pertinent to investigations into child sexual abuse with social services (Reeves et al., 2011). Procedural irregularities were also identified, suggesting that failings were not only attributable to the medical profession (Freeman, 1989). It could be argued that the persistent findings of subsequent reports identifying concerns about inter-professional working placed undue emphasis on this aspect of child protection and have resulted in an unhelpful bureaucratisation of procedures (Rupert, 2018). Muller (2019) evaluates the significance of openly shared information in assessing risk and provides a persuasive argument for the positive impact that greater inter-professional training has had on interagency working and indeed on the incidence of child deaths attributable to poor communication.

Paragraph two

Inter-professional working was identified as being a factor in failings in child protection investigations in the Butler-Sloss Inquiry (1988), the Climbié Report (2003) and the Laming Report (2009). The Butler-Sloss Inquiry identified inter-professional working and the risks posed by practitioners from different professions failing to share information effectively. It reported that medical practitioners failed to share information pertinent to investigations into child sexual abuse with social services (Reeves et al., 2011). Procedural irregularities were also identified (Freeman, 1989). Professionals from different professions do not always communicate effectively and this can be a cause of failings in assessing children at risk. The procedures governing child protection have increased and this has reduced the number of inquiries into child deaths (Rupert, 2018). There needs to be more inter-professional training and better communication between professionals.

(Continued)

(Continued)

Comment

How clear was it to you which paragraph was the more descriptive? Were you able to identify why? The words and phrases that give a clue to a more analytical way of writing include the following:

- important
- significant
- suggesting
- it could be argued
- undue
- resulted in an unhelpful
- provides a persuasive argument
- attributable to

The use of these words or phrases do not alone make your writing more analytical or structured around an argument, but they can be a useful prompt to make sure that you are evaluating and thinking about the significance of the evidence that you use, rather than just describing it. Moving from descriptive to analytical writing based around taking a position requires you to begin to put yourself, the writer and scholar, into your writing. This is the aspect of writing that will be considered next.

Developing your scholarly voice

Writing is a form of communication and writing an essay involves you in using a range of thinking – or cognitive – skills which are then communicated to your reader. Developing confidence in using your own scholarly voice takes time, but it is important in order to write an essay in which you are crafting an argument based on taking a position on the topic. Even when an essay is mainly descriptive you, as the writer, will be using scholarly skills beyond just reading and writing. The word 'scholarly' means activity related to academic study, so your scholarly voice is the voice you use when you are talking and writing about academic topics using an academic style. Your scholarly voice may be very different from the voice you use at home or even as a practitioner – you may use different vocabulary and you will certainly use evidence and both your own ideas and those of others in a more formal way than you would outside of academic or professional contexts. Some of the cognitive skills that are needed before and while you write include:

- interpreting the question and guidance;
- searching for relevant reading and keeping careful records of sources;
- taking notes and organising them around the themes or developing arguments to respond to the question;
- planning themes, key points and structure;
- synthesising reading and honing down what evidence to use;
- formulating the arguments and matching with supporting evidence.

This process is rarely linear – you are likely to move back and forth between these activities, reading, thinking, note-taking, planning, synthesising and re-planning. The reading, thinking and planning of an essay is likely to take at least as long, if not longer, than the writing. Your ability to undertake these thinking tasks will be reflected in the quality of your scholarly voice.

It is common for less experienced students to rely heavily on the reading they have done and many struggle to put the ideas in their own words, particularly when you find the reading difficult to understand. Everyone encounters reading that is challenging, whatever the level of study, but it is important to take your time to read slowly and make notes in your own words rather than highlighting or copying from a book or journal article. Practising writing notes from your reading in your own words is a good way to practise developing your scholarly voice without the risk of writing for an assessed task.

Activity 3.4

1. Read a chapter or an article, something that is relevant for an assignment or one of your current modules would be helpful. Read the whole piece through from beginning to end to get a sense of it. Start reading again and then stop after the first couple of pages and put away the reading so you are not tempted to refer to it.
2. Write down everything you can remember – it can be in bullet points, a diagram or written in sentences. Capture what you remember as the main points in whatever way is easiest for you. Don't be tempted to check back with the reading until you have noted down everything you can remember.
3. Once you have finished writing check your notes against the reading. The aim is not to reproduce the original but to capture the main points in your own words. When you compare your notes with the reading, make a note of anything important you missed and correct any errors, but try to resist copying any sections in the original wording.

Comment

You may find that this method of note-taking is very time-consuming at first, but you will get faster and some readings will be easier than others. The advantage of this approach is not only that you check that you have understood your reading, but you will avoid the risk of unintentionally plagiarising by copying original wording in your notes and then using this in your essay without acknowledging it as a direct quotation. Plagiarism and academic conduct are further discussed in the next section.

Using evidence and safe academic conduct

As discussed above it is important for the argument that you develop in an essay to be based on evidence, generally from your reading. While it is important to develop your own voice, a *scholarly* voice needs to demonstrate your ability to reason based on published and valid sources rather than on your own opinion only. Many students find the requirements around using evidence and referencing confusing and anxiety-provoking. Universities take academic conduct very seriously and you will be able to find guidance from your own course on both academic conduct and the required method of referencing.

Academic conduct is a general term that refers to following the expected rules relating to your academic study, but specifically is used in relation to plagiarism. Plagiarism is the use of content which has been written by someone else without permission or acknowledgement. This could include any of the following:

- copying all or some of another students work;
- purchasing an essay and passing all or part of it off as your own original work;
- using content from a published source (such as a book, article or website) in your own words without providing an acknowledgement of the source and a full reference;
- lifting words directly from a published source (such as a book, article or website) and failing to provide a full reference.

It can be confusing that you are required to use ideas and facts from published sources but that these should be in your own words or in the form of a short quotation. Whether you use a direct quotation or put content into your own words a reference should always be given. Detailed guidance on referencing is not provided here as there are several methods of referencing, such as the Harvard method, and your own university will give you guidance on the method that is required. All methods will require you to include a short reference in the body of the essay (an in-text citation) and then also full details at the end of your work (a reference list). Failure to include a reference can result in very serious penalties so it is very important that you seek advice if you are unclear about how to acknowledge and reference the sources you have used correctly.

Links to practice

Assignments which are directly related to practice will be discussed in Chapters 4 and 5, but there can be an overlap between academic essays and practice on social work programmes. The ways in which social work programmes are constructed differ from university to university. On some you will study some of your modules alongside sociology, psychology, social policy or even law students. The assignments for these modules are unlikely to require you to link your essay directly to practice. You will also study some modules which are very closely associated with practice, and some programmes will require all of your assignments to be applied in some way to social work practice. The inclusion of practice links, whether applying your discussion to a practice context generally or reflecting on your own direct practice while on placement, may shift the way in which you are expected to write your essay. One important difference is the use of the first person rather than writing in a passive voice. In simple terms writing in the first person means the use of the pronoun 'I', so for instance the example of an introduction above would be written as follows in the first person:

In this essay I will explore the benefits and challenges of inter-professional working in social work, drawing on the example of child protection. I will outline the concerns raised in public reports about the effectiveness of inter-professional working, including the Seebohm Report 1968, the Butler-Sloss Inquiry 1988 and the Victoria Climbié Inquiry 2003: Inquiry Report. I will outline the benefits of inter-professional working in the context of my practice in child protection, with reference to the principles of the Children Act 1989. I will analyse the persisting challenges of collaborating across agencies, including differing organisational cultures and methods of communication. Finally, with reference to Muller (2019) and French (2017), I will offer some strategies for enhancing the effectiveness of inter-professional working.

The meaning is essentially unchanged, but using the first person allows the writer to discuss their own reflections and practice more easily. The use of the first person will be explored in more detail in subsequent chapters, but at this point it is just important to be aware that different modules, even within one programme, may have different requirements around whether you write in the passive voice or the first person.

Why are essays helpful for social workers?

On the surface it can seem as if the academic essay has little in common with the kinds of writing that social workers undertake in practice. Research which explored the relationship between academic writing and practice writing revealed that there are in face some important commonalties and that learning to write academic essays can help students to develop and practise cognitive skills which can be applied to writing in practice (Rai and Lillis, 2013).

Activity 3.5

Look back at the list of cognitive processes which are involved in essay writing and think about how these might apply to writing in social work practice. Can you think of any parallels?

Cognitive process	Parallel activity in practice writing
Interpreting the question and guidance	
Searching for relevant reading and keeping careful records of sources	
Taking notes and organising them around the themes or developing arguments to respond to the question	
Planning themes, key points and structure	
Synthesising reading and honing down what evidence to use	
Formulating the arguments and matching with supporting evidence	

(Continued)

(Continued)

Comment

While the form, appearance and function of an essay may be very different from writing in practice, many of the cognitive processes are the same. Much of the writing undertaken in practice has detailed guidance on how it should be written. Reports and assessments in particular require the writer to undertake careful research, collecting evidence such as from service users, carers and other professionals and carefully recording the sources. Writing in practice needs to be accessible and easy to read, often under time pressures, so the ability to synthesise information and put it into your own words succinctly is very important. Finally, practice writing is frequently rhetorical, in other words its purpose is to put forward an argument based on evidence. Rhetorical or persuasive writing will be explored in more detail in the following chapters in Part One of this book.

Chapter summary

In this chapter we have explored the nature of the essay and why essays differ in particular disciplines. We have considered the process of developing an essay, including gathering your evidence, making notes and planning your structure and argument. Finally we have reflected on the relevance of essays to social work practice, a theme which you will encounter again in the Part Two of this book.

Further reading

Bottomley, J, Cartney, P and Pryjmachuk, S (2018) *Academic Writing and Referencing for Your Social Work Dregree.* St Albans: Critical Publishing

This book is designed for social work students and addresses the process of essay writing, including planning, structuring and developing an argument. There is also detailed guidance on referencing, although you should refer to the guidance at your own university for referencing style.

Roberts, J (2017) *Essentials of Essay Writing: What Markers Look For.* London: Palgrave.

This book looks at the purpose of essays and provides some very useful insights into what markers look for. It is a generic book rather than one aimed at social work students but covers issues such as interrogating the guidance and using evidence in building arguments.

4

Reflective writing

Introduction

Reflective writing can take many forms and is used in formative and summative assessment. This chapter will explore the benefits of reflective writing, its relevance to social work learning and also its limitations as a tool of assessment. The differences between reflective writing and essays will be identified, while also recognising that assignments presented as 'essays' may include a requirement for some reflection. The chapter will include discussion of the emotive aspect of reflective writing, particularly in the context of sensitive experiences.

What is reflective writing?

Reflective writing is frequently used as a form of assessment in social work, in common with other professional disciplines such as nursing and education. Reflective writing can take many forms and assignments may not always be named specifically as 'reflective'. This means that you need to read not only the title of the assignment but also the guidance in order to be clear about whether reflection is a required element and how this changes the way in which you are expected to write. In simple terms, reflection in academic writing means that you are expected to think and write about your own experiences – this might be based on your practice, your life experience and your values. Assessment types that would commonly require reflective writing include:

- reflective essays
- reflective journals or logs
- critical incident analyses
- practice studies.

The common element in any assessed task involving reflection is that you will be required to include content which is based on your own personal reflections alongside discussion and analysis of reading or theory. The way in which you present such reflections will vary considerably based on your own course and university, but the use of the word 'reflection' should signal to you that you may be expected to write a little differently from the way in which you would write, for example, an essay or report.

Activity 4.1 Why is reflective writing important in social work?

Spend a few moments jotting down some notes on why you think reflection is important in social work. Is this something you have used in your previous studies and how do you feel about using it now?

Comment

Reflection is an important tool in social work education and practice. Studying social work is as much about learning to become a practitioner as it is about academic study, and reflection enables you to make connections between your academic learning and your practice. This application of theoretical learning to practice can be challenging for many students and reflection is one of the ways in which students can both practise this skill and also demonstrate that they are able to transfer their learning. Reflection has deep roots in social work, arising from the early influences of psychoanalytic theory (Duncan-Daston and Schneller, 2016). Psychoanalytic theory derives from the work of Sigmund Freud and in very simple terms it foregrounds the significance of emotion and historical (conscious and unconscious) memories on current behaviour and experience. A full discussion of psychotherapy is beyond the scope of this book, but psychoanalytic-based therapy encourages reflection on past experiences, with a particular emphasis on the emotional impact, in order to gain a greater insight into current events, behaviour and interactions. There is a fuller discussion of the psychoanalytic and psychosocial theories which are relevant to reflective writing below, but for now it is just important to understand that there is a long historical tradition in social work of using reflection on events, including both emotional and cognitive responses to those events, to understand, learn and plan future practice.

Elements of reflective writing and their theoretical roots

Reflection is used as a learning tool both in practice and at university and is also commonly used in professional supervision for students and qualified social workers. As a student and practitioner in the 1980s I was required to undertake 'process recording', a method of reflection through writing structured accounts of a specific practice encounter which included both descriptive detail of what happened but also an account of the thoughts and feelings associated with the encounter. Process recording involves writing a very detailed narrative based on observation of the encounter, including as much detail as the practitioner can recall. You will explore process recording in more detail in Chapter 10.

This kind of reflective recording is a valuable learning tool just through the process of writing it, but its value is greatest when shared and discussed within a supervision or mentoring relationship. Process recording could be described as a form of professional 'therapy' with the aim of supporting practitioners to reflect critically and to take note of feelings and potentially subconscious responses which might provide useful insights into more effective practice. With the declining popularity of psychoanalytic practice in the UK process recording is less common now, but it is still used elsewhere, for example in Australia (Karpetis, 2019) and the United States (Papell, 2015) and has great value when used by supervisors or mentors who have been trained in this approach. It is a very time-consuming activity and has, as a result, been unpopular with some students but nonetheless offers a unique learning tool in social work education (Papell, 2015).

In the UK while process recording is rarely required, written reflections remain important learning tools through, for example, critical incident reports, reflective logs, journals and assessed reflective writing, which can be referred to as reflective essays or reports. All of these forms of writing involve learning through reflection and draw on a range of psychoanalytic, psychosocial and educational concepts. While the precise requirements of any reflective writing task will vary depending on the course and university, there are some common elements which have much in common with process recording.

Research Summary

As suggested above, there are a number of theoretical influences on reflective writing deriving from psychoanalytic, psychosocial and educational theories. Common to all of these is a recognition that there is an educational value in thoughtfully revisiting (practice) experiences in order to deepen learning and develop future practice. Most approaches also recognise the significance of recognising emotional responses to incidents and also the importance of applying knowledge such as theory and policies. One of the most commonly used tools for structuring reflection is Gibbs's reflective cycle (1988) which is illustrated in Figure 4.1.

Gibbs's reflective cycle is used extensively as a tool for learning, particularly in the context of nursing practice, although it is also applicable to social work practice. The cycle has many similarities with process recording in that a description is followed by a

(Continued)

(Continued)

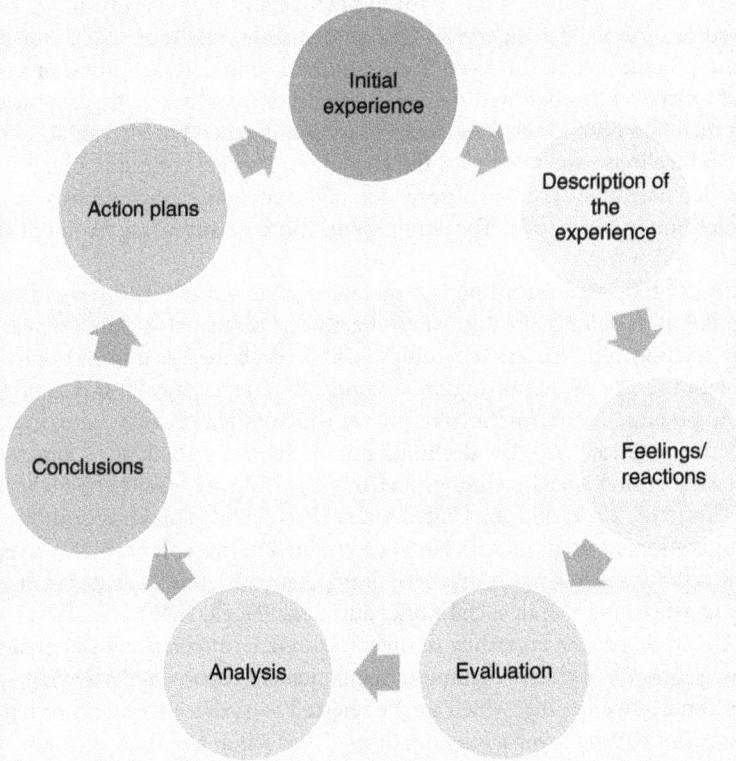

Figure 4.1 Gibbs's reflective cycle (adapted from Gibbs, 1988)

reflection on the emotions and feelings generated. The original intention of Gibbs's approach was to structure a debriefing process which acknowledged the impact of emotion on practice. The emphasis on emotion has lessened now as the model is now used as a relatively simple tool to aid individual reflection and had been criticised for not taking into account the wider structural and contextual issues which impact on practice (Middleton, 2017). Process recording also focuses on individual practice rather than broader issues but it differs from Gibbs's cycle in its requirement for a detailed written account and presumption that a supervisor or mentor will work with the student to uncover unconscious responses, motivations or behaviours.

Another influential reflective model is that of Schön, an educationalist who argued that deep learning occurs when students are able to make connections between their practice and their learning. Schön developed the important concepts of 'reflection-in-action' and 'reflection-on-action'. Reflection-in-action refers to the process of reflecting and modifying practice during a practice event in real time, while reflection-on-action takes place after the practice event and so informs future practice and allows more time for analysis (Schön, 1983).

All of the approaches to reflection discussed here have the potential to be used within a learning conversation, as is intended with process recording. Ryding and Wernersson

(2019) suggest that individual self-reflection can assist practitioners understand and evaluate the application of theory and values to their practice but that reflection can offer an even richer learning experience when it takes place within a supervisory relationship. Where reflection takes the form of a conversation there are opportunities for a greater level of challenge, critical analysis and consideration of systems, contexts and interrelationships that may be difficult for a practitioner to access when reflecting in isolation. There is a risk, therefore, that some of the rich potential offered by reflection can be lost if it is only used as an assessment tool base on a relatively rigid and simple model rather than the basis for an exploratory learning conversation.

Reflection and assessment

It is common for reflection to be required as an element of assessed writing, but as suggested above reflection offers a rich learning experience irrespective of its being an assessment task. In fact Boud (1999) argues that reflection should not be assessed due to inherent contradictions:

> *Assessment involves putting forward one's best work . . . Reflection, on the other hand, is about exploration, understanding, questioning, probing discrepancies and so on. There is always a danger that assessment will obliterate the very practices of reflection which courses aim to promote.*

> (Boud, 1999, p123)

Boud highlights here one of the central challenges for assessing reflection. Reflection often explicitly requires students to recognise and acknowledge ways in which their practice could be improved. This developmental aspect of reflection is illustrated in Gibbs's reflective cycle in which analysis and conclusions are followed by an 'action plan'. This implied requirement to identify a 'failing' which needs improvement is made more challenging by the tendency for reflective models to encourage students to primarily focus on their own individual practice rather than wider organisational, institutional or interrelational factors. Students' natural desire to maximise their success in assessments may also encourage them to construct problematic practice in order to offer 'reflective' solutions or improvements to inform their action planning. The following case study is from a student who participated in research that I undertook with second-year social work students.

Case Study

David

David was an unqualified social worker sponsored by his employer. David was a mature student on the social work degree and completed his first degree in politics after following a traditional route into higher education from school. As an academically able student,

(Continued)

(Continued)

David had little difficulty with the academic assignments on his social work degree and was consistently gaining high marks in all but his reflective assignments. David was very frustrated by the lower grades that he was receiving for his reflective assignments, which were a core element of the modules focusing on practice. He was aware that the guidance on the reflective assignments differed from the more traditional essays that he was used to. He felt very frustrated, however, that based on his experience the guidance on the reflective assignments were encouraging him to write in a way which he did not consider to be 'academic'. This included writing in the first person, using description of his practice and personal experiences and offering reflections which included discussion of his feelings and values. David also felt very frustrated that he needed to provide examples of ways in which he could improve his practice, or do things differently in the future. While he was sometimes able to offer genuine suggestions for how he could improve his practice, this was not always the case and he felt under pressure to write about examples of bad, or at least less than best, practice in order to meet the assignment brief. Feedback on David's reflective assignments from a panel of tutors who reviewed it anonymously for the research project suggested that David's work was 'defensively academic' and one tutor commented that:

> The student writes almost as an intelligent observer rather than someone who will have to go in to work tomorrow and make decisions based on values, amongst other things. For me, this conflicts with competence-based models of assessment.

Half of the tutor panel graded it as a fail or near fail. In reality David did not fail any of his assignments and comfortably qualified as a social worker. The difference in grades between the 'essays' and the 'reflective' assignments was a source of frustration for him as not only did they pull down his overall grade but he perceived them as being unhelpful for his learning as they seemed to require him to fabricate practice examples to reflect on in order to meet the assignment requirement. David had no difficulty reflecting on and discussing his practice in the context of face-to-face discussions with his workplace supervisor. The difficulties arose because the reflective writing was presented as 'academic writing' when David did not consider it to be so and was assessed based on a requirement to identify practice that needed to be improved.

David's experience may not be typical but it is not unusual either. If you have completed a degree course which involved writing essays prior to studying for your social work degree you may recognise at least some of his experiences. On some social work courses reflective writing assignments may not differ so significantly from essay format assignments but the focus on experience and identifying changes in practice are common features of reflective writing. While it is important to remember that there are significant differences in expectations between universities and courses, Table 4.1 broadly signals some of the *typical* differences between an 'essay' and 'reflective writing'.

There are of course many similarities between essays and reflective writing, although on some courses the distinction is less clear, for example the use of I may still be discouraged in a reflective assignment, perhaps with the exception of presenting a case study or reflective section. Some assignments will be referred to as 'reflective essays' but when planning your writing you should focus more on the guidance given on a specific assignment than the title of the assessment task as this can be misleading. The CAPS method is one way to make sure that you have understood what is required on a specific assignment and can therefore be very helpful when preparing for a reflective assignment. An illustration is offered in Table 4.2.

Table 4.1 Differences between an essay and reflective writing

Essay	Reflective writing
Discourages the use of I, me, my* (e.g 'This essay will . . .')	Encourages the use of I, me, my* ('In this essay I will . . .')
Focus is on creating an argument based on theory from published sources/reading	Focus is on demonstrating learning through applying theory to personal/practice experiences
Evidence is from published sources/reading only	Evidence is from published sources/reading and also examples of practice
Does not include personal/practice experience or observation	Requires reflection on personal/practice experience
Does not include any commentary on changes to future practice/learning	Requires the author to include commentary on changes to future practice/learning
Theory is used as the basis for critical analysis of a question or topic	Theory is applied to practice in order to critically evaluate the author's professional development
Sources are all published material and must be acknowledged	Sources from practice should be anonymised, published sources must be acknowledged
Impersonal and objective with a focus on dispassionate academic argument	Personal and often emotive content which includes discussion of values and feelings

*First person singular pronoun ('I concluded that . . .') as opposed to using a passive voice ('The conclusion was drawn that . . .').

Table 4.2 Example of the CAPS method

		Ask yourself . . .	Illustrative answer
C	Context	Which module is this assignment for? Does it include assessment of my practice and do the module learning outcomes include reflection or learning from practice?	This is a practice module and the learning outcomes include a requirement to demonstrate my ability to apply theory and values to practice and also to demonstrate my ability to reflect and develop my practice.
A	Audience	Who are you writing your assignment for? What should you assume about their expectations of your writing and the implications for how you should write?	The module lead who will be assessing my assignment. This person will have a good understanding of the theory I need to use but not a detailed understanding of the context of the practice I will draw on, so I need to make sure that I give enough detail to make my practice examples and reflections make sense.

(Continued)

Table 4.2 (Continued)

		Ask yourself . . .	Illustrative answer
P	Purpose	What is the main purpose of this assignment? Are there any secondary purposes that you need to bear in mind?	The main purpose is assessing my knowledge against the learning outcomes for the module. This includes my ability to apply my learning to practice. As a reflective assignment a secondary aim is to develop my own learning through the process of reflecting on my learning in order to develop my practice.
S	Self	Who am I writing as in this assignment? Which aspects of my identity are relevant?	I am writing as a student but also as a novice social work practitioner. I am also using reflection on my values and so, in the context of my practice in a children and families team, I will draw on my personal identity as a parent.

The responses to the CAPS question will vary and are very individual to you, your university, your course, the module you are writing for and the specific assignment on the module. The questions are just prompts to remind you to think carefully about these aspects of your writing. For reflective writing it is particularly important to think about the final question, that of self. As with all academic writing you will draw on your student self, but for reflective writing you will normally also draw on yourself as a novice social worker and often some very personal aspects of your identity, in the example here yourself as a practitioner. The very personal nature of reflective writing, together with the often highly emotive context of social work practice, means that reflective writing can be very sensitive. Emotion is not normally a very significant element of academic writing but it is an important element to be aware of when writing reflectively about practice. The role of emotion may or may not be recognised on the course you are studying or by your tutors, but you should still be aware of it as a student writer. The following case study illustrates one of the ways in which an awareness of the power of emotion is relevant to your writing but also the way in which you understand the feedback on your writing. This case study is drawn from Rai (2008).

Case Study

Patricia

Patricia was writing a reflective assignment based on her final placement on her social work degree. The assignment required her to reflect and apply theory to an example of her practice and identify what she had learnt from the reflection and how she would change her future practice as a result of her reflections. Patricia was working in an adult team linked to a hospital and she chose to write about her work with a woman called Ann who had received a sudden and unexpected terminal diagnosis. The woman had a husband and school age children. Patricia identified strongly with Ann, as she was a similar age and both had partners and children. Patricia wrote the following in her assignment.

> I have worked in partnership with Ann to gain her trust and to advocate on her behalf as she has tried to assimilate so much distressing information and navigate her way through unfathomable depths of loss – loss of independence, of dignity, of credibility and ultimately of life itself. I reflect that the strength of my support for Ann is largely as a result of the empathy I feel for her as she attempts to protect her values from being compromised. The positive identity, with which Ann was admitted to hospital, is being systematically undermined by the inference that she is unreasonable, unrealistic and difficult, basically because she has refused to conform. Individuals 'who are perceived as "difficult" appear to find it hard to take advantage of the opportunities for choice' [reference given]. In this instance Ann is being both labelled and discouraged from making an informed choice about where she feels her future care needs should be met.
>
> There have also been questions raised about Ann's competency in decision-making given the progressive nature of her illness. These are all issues with which I identify and I have during the past six weeks taken significant steps to protect both my personal privacy and my family should I ever be diagnosed with a life-limiting illness or meet an untimely death. I have made a will, identified potential guardians for my children, shared with a close friend the location of private documents, identified a responsible person who is prepared to take on Power of Attorney should it ever be necessary and I have disposed of anything incriminating. I feel that my involvement with Ann has given me a focus in terms of my own values. To help Ann to resolve some of the internal struggles she faces in respect of her impending death, it has been necessary for me to explore some of my own anxieties in terms of my own morbidity.

Patricia talked of finding this assignment very difficult to write as it took her back to the distressing experience of working with Ann and also reflecting on her own morbidity. She found it difficult to write about her feelings alongside the theory and analysis that she knew was required and talked about managing to do this by writing about the 'guts' (reflection on her feelings) separately from the 'academic stuff' (theory) and then bringing the two together afterwards. However, when Patricia received feedback on this assignment she experienced it as insensitive and upsetting. Her tutor suggested that she should reflect even more deeply on the impact of this experience on her personally but also explain more clearly how she would change her practice in future.

> I think it is worth reflecting upon the way in which this case helped you to effectively step into the service users' shoes in some ways – not completely of course, but share worries about the future, plans to be completed etc. clearly struck a chord with you and perhaps you are looking about how you have developed a way of coping with fears that we all have to some degree in a more conscious way. Remember that looking at change implies saying where you were before the situation arose – that would be useful to comment upon in the future in relation to writing about personal development.

(Continued)

(Continued)

While this feedback may have been consistent with the assignment brief and learning outcomes, the request to delve even deeper into very painful reflections within the context of assessed written work was difficult and frustrating for Patricia. This was in part because she felt she was being asked for even deeper disclosure of her personal feelings but also because it seemed to push her writing even further away from the essays which she was more familiar with. She commented on the feedback:

> *Well for this module you need 'I want, I think, I feel' whereas for the other module it is more writing in the passive voice. Well you write that for your auntie Jane don't you? You don't write it for a course!*

The case study based on Patricia's experiences raises some important considerations. Firstly both student and tutor should recognise the potential emotional impact of writing about sensitive practice experiences, particularly where there is an expectation of reflecting on these in the context of personal values and experiences. Reflective writing which requires or encourages this kind of self-disclosure can have a powerful impact on you as the writer, just as self-disclosure can be a powerful but potentially risky action in practice with service users. Rai (2012) draws on the work of Chelune (1979) who suggests that there are three variables which impact on the effectiveness of self-disclosure: the first is the normative value, in other words how commonplace is disclosure in a particular context; the second is the expressive value, which refers to the significance of the disclosed information to the teller; and the final variable is voluntariness, or in other words how much choice the teller has about whether and what to disclose. In the context of reflective writing in social work these variables could be considered as shown in Table 4.3.

Table 4.3 Variables in reflective writing

	Question to ask	Illustrative response	Impact
Normative value	How common is it to expect self-disclosure in this kind of writing?	In academic writing generally self-disclosure is very uncommon, but in social work practice it is more common although still treated with caution. An expectation of self-disclosure in reflective writing poses risks as it does not have a high normative value.	High
Expressive value	How emotionally sensitive is the information being shared?	There is a potential for shared information to have an extremely high expressive value as a result of the nature of much social work practice and the common expectation for students to relate practice to their own values and personal experiences.	High

	Question to ask	Illustrative response	Impact
Voluntariness	How much choice is there about whether and what is disclosed?	Where reflective writing requires self-disclosure within formative assessment (assessment which contributes to passing or failing the qualification or course) there is very little choice and so the impact is very high. The choice that a student may have is over the specific practice example chosen and the personal impact on them.	High

Self-disclosure can have an important place in social work writing, but as Chelune's analysis indicates, there is a risk of it having a high impact on the writer. As a result it should be treated with sensitivity and caution to ensure that it addresses its purpose without causing emotional harm.

Chapter summary

This chapter has explored the value of reflection and reflective writing in social work. We have considered some of the challenges of reflective writing and how you can apply CAPS before you begin a writing task to help you make your writing as effective as possible. The case study of Patricia illustrates the potential emotional impact of reflective writing and the care needed when engaging in writing, particularly when assessed, which is very sensitive. In Chapter 5 we will explore the challenges of creating portfolios, which often contain reflective writing.

Further reading

Rai, L (2006) Owning (up to) reflective writing in social work education, *Social Work Education*, 25(8): 785–797.

This is a short journal article which focuses specifically on reflective writing in social work.

Williams, K, Wooliams, J and Spiro, J (2020) *Reflective Writing*. London: Palgrave Macmillan.

This is a generic book on reflective writing so care needs to be taken when applying it to social work. It contains some useful ideas about using reflective thinking to improve your academic writing.

5
Writing about practice

Introduction

Practice learning is at the heart of social work education but there is very little published guidance on how to write about your practice. This chapter focuses on the ways
in which you will need to evidence your practice and why this is important. In the
previous chapter you considered the role of reflection in your writing, and this is also
important when providing evidence of your practice competence. The most substantial
document in which social work students write about practice is the portfolio which
evidences your competence in each practice placement. This chapter provides guidance
on how to compile a portfolio, what evidence to include and how to structure it so that
it is accessible for your readers and assessors. You will also learn about the benefits and
limitations of e-portfolios and the chapter ends with a consideration of how to maintain
confidentiality in your practice writing.

Why write about practice?

Social work education, in common with many professional programmes, teaches and assesses what can be referred to as both 'theoretical' and 'practice' learning. Assignments for some modules may include very little or no reference to practice, for example pure social science modules which might be shared with students on other programmes such as sociology, psychology or social policy. Many modules, however, will include practice either in the form of case studies, provided as part of the teaching, or through activities or assignments which ask you to reflect on your own practice experiences.

Drawing on theory to reflect on practice

The relationship between theory and practice has always been a complex and challenging aspect of social work education as it requires a careful integration of learning that takes place in practice with learning in university. This division of responsibility for teaching signals perhaps one of the greatest challenges of social work education, that of relating theory to practice. There have been presumptions that theory is taught at university while practice is taught on practice placements but the reality is less clear cut. From my own experience as an educator and practitioner, I am aware of long running debates about how to integrate the teaching of theory and practice between academics based in universities and practitioners involved in practice teaching. Social work educators in both settings have responsibilities for teaching and ultimately ensuring that graduates are safe and effective practitioners. University educators in social work have no statutory obligation to retain a role in practice (unlike nurse educators for example) and so may not have practised for many years. They do, however, need to teach the knowledge required for the social work curriculum and many will also be using this knowledge to inform their research. In contrast practice educators are working in practice alongside their support for students and for many the teaching role is very much a secondary activity, but theory routinely informs their practice.

Research Summary

Despite this implicit assumption about responsibilities or expertise in teaching, separating theory and practice is not a reflection of reality. The relationship between theory and practice has always been a complex and challenging one. Thompson (2017) challenges the idea that it is possible to practise without theory, referring to this as the 'fallacy of theoryless practice'. He suggests that all practice is based on theory. This may be informal or drawn from published work but in order for social workers to be able to reflect on a critique of their practice, they should be able to refer to a framework of ideas and values that has informed their practice. Part of the process of practice learning, therefore, is making the theory that underpins practice explicit, and this is particularly important in the context of written reflective assessments.

Activity 5.1

The following table lists some of the sources of what can broadly be referred to as 'theory' which might inform practice. Which of these would you categorise as 'formal' theory and which 'informal'? Would any of these not be suitable to use in a written assignment?

Source	Notes
Website, for example MENCAP or NSCPP	
Journal article	
Notes and handouts from a training session provided by your placement	
Case study provided by university	
Notes of a discussion with your practice educator	
Legislation	
Notes in a reflective journal	
Policy guidance provided by your placement	
Professional standards, for example from Social Work England	
Reflective conversations with peers	
Published book	
Codes of practice, for example published by the Scottish Social Services Council	
Professional Capabilities Framework	
Lecture notes	

Comment

This is not an exhaustive list of the potential sources of 'knowledge' that might inform your practice, but it illustrates both the variety of potential sources and the breadth of the formal/informal spectrum. When using sources of evidence in your assessed writing it is always important to acknowledge the source, but failing to correctly reference 'formal' sources will be treated as an 'academic offence' which can attract a serious penalty. As discussed in Chapters 1 and 2 you should refer to the specific guidance provided by your university on how to reference published sources, such as books, journal articles, legislation and websites. Reference to informal, or less formal, sources such as documents within your practice agency, from training sessions or discussions with peers or colleagues, can be less clear and you should check with your tutor about whether it is acceptable to include these and how to acknowledge them.

Portfolios of practice

It is common for the assessment of practice to include the submission of a portfolio. The purpose of a practice portfolio is to demonstrate your competence in practice, normally through a collection of evidence required by your programme. It is usually a substantial element of assessment and includes a report from your practice educator with a recommendation of the outcome of your placement assessment. The requirements of each programme will differ so it is important to access and make sure that you understand the specific requirements of your own programme of study. If you undertake more than one placement you are likely to be required to produce a portfolio for each of them, and the requirements may differ.

What should be included in a portfolio?

Generally a portfolio is a collection of written evidence, some of which will have been written by you as the student and some of which will have been written by other people who can testify to the quality of your practice. Typical documents that may be included in portfolios are:

- a report making a recommendation written by your practice educator, often referred to as a 'practice assessment report';
- records of your practice or case summaries which may include reflective discussion of your practice;
- examples of your practice writing – this might include extracts from case recordings, reports or emails;
- testimonials or feedback from service users;
- testimonials or feedback from colleagues who have observed your practice;
- observations of your practice by your practice educator or a nominated colleague;
- a mapping document demonstrating where and how you have met the requirements of the programme and the evidence in the portfolio that supports this. These requirements differ depending on the national professional standards where you are studying, but in England these would be the BASW Professional Capabilities Framework and the Social Work England Professional Standards for Social Workers in England;
- a confirmation of practice learning days completed;
- supervision notes.

Activity 5.2

Some of the documents in a portfolio will be examples of your own practice writing, selected and collated to provide evidence of your practice competence. Other documents have been written specifically for the purpose of your practice assessment, either by you or by someone who has observed or experienced your practice. Using a table like the one provided here, itemise the types of document that your programme requires you to include in your portfolio:

Practice documents included as evidence of your competence	e.g. case recording
Documents written by you as a student	e.g. reflective case summary
Documents written by someone who has observed or experienced your practice	e.g. practice educator report

The balance of documents in each category will be different depending on the programme that you are studying for. Some universities place the main responsibility on practice educators to map the evidence against the assessment criteria through their report; others will expect students to take most of the responsibility for compiling evidence to demonstrate their competence, which is then signed off and confirmed by the practice educator. Regardless of the guidelines on how a portfolio should be collated and presented, the responsibility for identifying and gathering evidence throughout the practice placement is shared between the student, the practice educator and, to a lesser extent, the university tutor who has responsibility for overseeing the quality of the placement. Any gaps in evidence, whether resulting in a lack of practice opportunities or concerns about a student's developing competence in a specific area should be identified as early as possible so that this can be discussed and resolved through an action plan in good time. This process is normally managed through meetings between the student, practice educator and a tutor from the university at the beginning, middle and end of the placement.

Portfolios are commonly assessed by at least two people, one representing practice agencies and one representing the university. Assessors may have a large number of portfolios to read, and it is unlikely that they will read every document contained in the portfolio word by word. Many of the documents are included as evidence of your practice to support the assessment made by your practice educator. As such the documents themselves will not be assessed, but they will be checked to ensure that they do in fact provide the evidence that has been claimed.

Activity 5.3

Have another look at the table you completed for the Activity 5.2 and in a new column identify which documents are broadly 'evidence' and which are broadly 'assessed' as follows:

		Evidence	Assessed
Practice documents included as evidence of your competence	e.g. case recording	X	
Documents written by you as a student	e.g. reflective case summary		X
Documents written by someone who has observed or experienced your practice	e.g. practice educator report	X	

A practice educator's report could be argued to be an additional category as it is not strictly evidence or assessed, but rather offers an assessment of your practice based on evidence. Other examples of evidence would include testimonials from service users or colleagues and any other practice writing that is included in the portfolio such as reports or correspondence.

Clarity and organisation

It is important when compiling a portfolio to ensure that it is well organised and clear for the reader to follow. Portfolios often contain a large number of documents and the total word count across all of these documents can be very high. Reading and assessing portfolios is a time-consuming and sometimes very difficult task, but as you saw in Activity 5.3 some of the documents are included as evidence and so are not directly assessed. The people assessing your portfolio will therefore read your assessment items in a similar way to other academic assignments, but the documents included as evidence will be checked rather than assessed. The assessor will be checking that the documents included are relevant to the claim made for them (by you or your practice educator) and that it provides sufficient evidence of your competence against a particular standard. It is important, therefore, that you select the best evidence that you have available to you but also that you organise your portfolio as clearly as possible so that you make the task for the assessor as easy as you can.

Your university may give you a template or structure to organise your portfolio, and if this is the case you should follow this carefully. If you are required to organise your own portfolio the following guidance should ensure that your portfolio is easy for your assessor to negotiate and assess.

1. Make sure that your portfolio is securely bound so that pages cannot fall out and either become lost or replaced in the wrong order. Remember that your portfolio may need to be transported or passed to more than one assessor.
2. Provide a clear index which lists every item in order, ideally with page or section numbers.
3. Your name and any student identification number should be clearly marked on the portfolio and ideally included as a header on all documents just in case pages become separated from the portfolio.
4. The most important documents in your portfolio are your practice educator report, which will include a recommendation, and your own reports or reflective logs. These documents should come first and be clearly marked.
5. Most portfolios will require you to 'map' your evidence against the standards that you are required to meet. This may be included in your practice assessors report, in your own report or in a separate mapping document. Follow the guidelines given to you carefully to ensure that the mapping is complete, that any evidence referred to is actually included in the portfolio and that any standards that have not been met or where evidence is missing are explained.
6. Portfolios commonly require you to include a document which confirms the number of placement days that you have completed, so check that this is included and accurate.
7. For any writing that you include, such as a reflective account or record, make sure that you follow the same protocols for academic referencing of any published sources used that are required for other academic assignments.
8. Check that any documents that require signature are actually signed and dated as required.
9. Check that all documents included in your portfolio are fully anonymised (see the section on confidentiality below).
10. Think about the best way to present your portfolio so that it is easy to use the index to find information quickly. For example, think about using coloured dividers or sticky tabs/index tabs on each section.

Finally a good way to check that your portfolio will be easy to navigate is to use the mapping document to find each item of evidence yourself, as if you were the assessor. If you can swap with another student this will be an even more helpful check that other people will be able to find their way around your portfolio. Remember that, however good your practice and your evidence, assessors will need to be able to find the relevant documents to check them, and an assessor who is frustrated by hunting through a chaotic portfolio may not be in the best mindset to assess your competence.

e-Portfolios

It is increasingly common for programmes to provide an online platform for portfolios to be submitted as digital documents. There is no universal platform for submitting an e-portfolio but if this is the system used at your university you will be given guidance on which platform to submit through and how to use it. The use of e-portfolios can make it much easier to share and store and, where a good tool is used, to organise your portfolio. There are, however, some challenges to using e-portfolios in social work education. For example, e-portfolios will require all of the component documents to be available digitally and in a file type that is compatible with the platform being used. This is not always possible when you are required to include documents from your practice such as assessment reports or correspondence which are likely to have been written on agency systems which are protected and may not be in a file format compatible with the e-portfolio platform.

There are also great benefits from e-portfolios as tools to help you collate and make sense of your learning both during your studies and as preparation for ongoing Personal Development Planning (PDP) and Continuing Professional Development (CPD). PDP is a live record of your developing skills, study and career plans and is commonly a task included in undergraduate studies. CPD refers to the ongoing learning and development that social workers, along with many other professions, are required to complete throughout their career to keep knowledge and skills up to date. CPD is a requirement of joining the professional workforce and social workers are required to evidence their ongoing CPD as part of renewing their registration (Social Work England, 2019). There can be some overlap between PDP and CPD and your PDP can become the foundation for your CPD once you qualify (Bottomley et al., 2018). Some undergraduate e-portfolio platforms offer a free alumni account which can support the transition from education to professional development in practice. Entering the workforce will bring not only professional requirements, but also requirements from your employer.

Care delivered by social workers is in a state of constant change and individuals have a responsibility to ensure that their own practice is based on sound knowledge and understanding and on good research where this exists. While employers have an obligation to provide some training and development and support for CPD, the responsibility lies mainly with you as the practitioner, so you need to define your own needs, which in turn will improve the quality of care for service users as the individual will be knowledgeable and up to date with current effective practice.

As with paper-based portfolios, e-portfolios can support recording experiences, reflective learning, peer review and action planning for development. An electronic format also allows you to make links to evidence in different file formats, such as video and audio files, and some platforms allow items to be collated into a presentation format. Evidence might include conversations or observations with a colleague, which might be video or audio recordings, a critical incident in the workplace or a formal certificated training course. You can also record something in the portfolio and keep it private – you are in control of each record you create and can choose to share any item with a colleague for comment or at an appropriate point you can include it as evidence of your competence. The ability to collate and share documents prior to submitting an assessment can provide more flexibility than a paper portfolio. Paper portfolios can be weighty items, particularly when they are in draft as it can be helpful to save several examples of a particular kind of evidence (Reed, 2015). An electronic format means that individual elements (or the whole portfolio) can be shared contemporaneously with several people, such as your tutor, line manager or practice educator.

Case Study

Amrit

Amrit is a second-year social work student and had the option of submitting his final portfolio as hard copy or using an electronic platform. He decided to use the electronic platform as he had already collected and saved a lot of documents digitally on his first placement and thought this might give him more flexibility. He was also working with people with learning disabilities on his second placement and wanted to try to gather some service user feedback as audio recordings. Amrit was confident using IT and interested in exploring ways to make his portfolio richer as well as keen to get feedback on his developing portfolio throughout his placement. He discussed this with his tutor and practice educator and both were happy with this approach.

Amrit, his tutor and practice educator all found using an e-portfolio a really effective way to work. Amrit found it easier to gather evidence as he went and not worry too much about what would go into the final portfolio until he was due to submit it for assessment. His tutor found it useful to view examples of evidence – it gave her a better insight into his placement and she was able to advise on what would be most useful for his assessment. His practice educator worked closely with Amrit to find ways to collect good examples of his practice and helped him find ways to create audio recordings of service user feedback which were ethically sound and preserved confidentiality.

Within an e-portfolio a user can use templates to provide structure to the recording process. This helps guide individuals through recording their activities, promotes reflection on the learning and helps highlight how it has influenced their practice. Using an e-portfolio system that provides templates to scaffold learning and recording can be of particular benefit to those who find it difficult to begin the recording process on a blank screen. Once recorded, items can be revisited, reflected upon and collated to provide a comprehensive portfolio of activity.

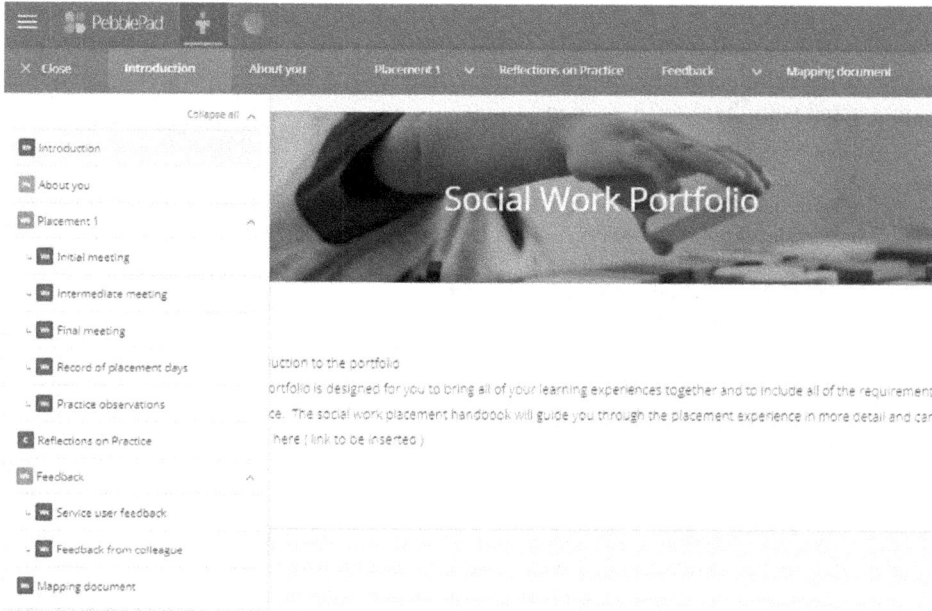

Figure 5.1 Example of an e-portfolio for social workers in training (provided by PebblePad © 2020. Reproduced with permission).

Social workers learn and develop in the workplace on a daily basis. They are, however, frequently time-pressured resulting in CPD evidence sometimes being recorded in retrospect, particularly if at the time of the learning event the purpose is not obvious or it feels like a tick-box exercise. Learning recorded in an e-portfolio can be reviewed and used again for multiple purposes, including evidencing CPD, while appraisals and job applications give individuals the maximum benefit from their efforts. Recording activities and experiences is an opportunity to develop the skills of critical analysis, a crucial element of professional competency and an opportunity to relate theory to practice.

Social work requires you to deliver safe, good-quality care and risk management procedures will exist as part of the quality assurance mechanisms employed by the service providers. Having a personal space as part of a portfolio system where you can explore your practice and then share this confidentially for guidance and support can assist with your reflections on your own practice and that of the agency more broadly. At some time during your career you may be identified by management or their professional body as needing to develop their practice and will be actively encouraged to pursue and evidence CPD around particular outcomes. In a few cases there may be a Fitness to Practice issue that is dealt with by the professional body responsible for the registrant and often the outcome identifies a need to develop practice through CPD and reflective practice, and to provide evidence of this to the professional body and the employer. Having a personal space within a portfolio system to develop this and share progress with others can be a positive developmental tool. A portfolio containing records of learning, reflective insights into practice and logs of activity can provide clear evidence that a practitioner has made an effort to improve their practice and maintain their cultural competence within the workplace. These can be further evidenced by testimony and comment from others who have supported, guided and interacted with them during the process.

Things that a qualified social worker could record in their e-portfolio:

- reflection on CPD study days and activities
- CPD evidence for registration
- standards of social work profession
- feedback from service users and other professionals
- supervision reflections
- practice educators can record their activities with their students
- evidence of research in practice
- personal development plan
- appraisal.

While individual items are important, evidence is of more value, such as creating a narrative around experiences and planning for future practice. This kind of development tells a story about your learning journey, which is life-long and life-wide. Capturing these kinds of experience within an e-portfolio can make effective use of time and resources for busy professionals.

Confidentiality

Whether a portfolio is collated electronically or in hard copy it is imperative that confidentiality is meticulously preserved. A portfolio, or any other assessed document which makes reference to practice, can be automatically failed if there are breaches of confidentiality. If the breach is considered serious then the university may consider taking disciplinary action or reviewing a student's progress under professional suitability policies. When addressing confidentiality you should consider service users but also ensure that specific services and locations are anonymised. There are a number of ways in which you can anonymise names and places, depending on the type of document you are writing. Documents which you are writing yourself for the purpose of assessment, such as reflective essays, records of practice or case summaries, can be anonymised by using one of the formats in Table 5.1.

Table 5.1 Illustration of options for anonymising a family, home address and school

Real name	Helen Goodge			
Anonymised options		Service user 1	Service user A	Kim Smith
Real name	Robert Goodge			
Anonymised options		Service user 2	Service user B	George Smith

Real name	Billy Goodge			
Anonymised options		Child 1	Child A	Tommy Smith
Real home address	24 York Place, Leeds			
Anonymised options		Location 1	Location A	Hightown
Real school name	Castleton Primary School			
Anonymised options		School 1	School A	Hightown Primary School

It can be helpful for the reader to stick to one system of anonymising names (so don't combine 'service user 1' with made-up names) but it is also important to signal members of the same family if your document refers to more than one service user or family. If you decide to use names rather than 'service user 1, 2, 3,' etc., you should not rely on this to indicate to the reader that names have been anonymised. In the illustration above you will see that names chosen are intended to be obviously fabricated, but you should also include a clear statement that all names and places have been fully anonymised. Most universities will require you to sign a statement to this effect prior to submitting your work.

If you need to include evidence which is a copy of a practice document then it can be more tricky to anonymise as you may not be able to edit the original electronically. Ideally you should copy the document into a different digital format which you can edit, for example cut and paste to a Word document. This is sometimes not possible, for example if the original is a PDF or other format you are not able to edit offline. If this is the case you will need to print off the document and anonymise by hand and then scan it to upload as a digital document again. You may need to seek advice from IT support in your placement on the best way to edit an electronic document downloaded from your agency's recording systems.

Chapter summary

In this chapter we have explored the different ways in which you may be required to write about your practice. The importance of evidence, reflection and linking theory to practice has been highlighted. We have looked in some detail at the practice portfolio and ways to structure this effectively, whether as paper or e-portfolio. The affordances of e-portfolios have been explored, including the value of being able to share and obtain feedback from others as you develop your evidence. Finally we have considered the vital issue of confidentiality and ways in which you can maintain this while also ensuring that your writing is clear for the reader.

Further reading

There is very little published specifically on writing about practice in social work but if you use the index you will find some references in the following books:

Bottomley, J, Cartney, P and Prymanchuck, S (2018) *Studying for Your Social Work Degree.* St Albans: Critical Publishing.

This is a generic book about studying for your social work degree and is very accessible. If you search you will find a few references to creating portfolios.

Parker, J (2010) *Effective Practice Learning in Social Work.* Exeter: Learning Matters.

This book provides a very good overview of learning in practice generally, and contains a chapter on assessment of practice, gathering evidence and demonstrating competence.

6

Writing about research

Introduction

So far we have looked at academic writing in the form of essays, reflective writing and portfolios. Social work students and social workers may also write about research in a number of contexts, including for assessment. In this chapter we will consider what is meant by research in social work and the range of types of research activity and the associated texts that you may be required to write. Students are not generally required to undertake research unless they are studying for postgraduate qualifications but it is important for students at all levels to be able to appraise research reports. The elements of a research report will be reviewed and you will have an opportunity to evaluate some research papers from different sources.

What is research?

The word research is used in many ways. You may be asked as a student to undertake 'research' in preparation for writing an assignment but you may also be asked to use or cite 'research' in your writing or your practice. In general terms, research refers to a systematic investigation in order to produce new knowledge. The differences between different kinds of research arise from the methods used to gather evidence and the originality of the new knowledge produced. Depending on the type and purpose of research being conducted it may include the following elements.

Research questions

Research questions are the basis for designing any research. They are the questions that a researcher plans to try and answer through their research. It is important that research questions are sufficiently focused, clear and precise to be answered through the planned research. Research would commonly be based on more than one question but not more than three or four.

An example of related research questions would be:

1. *How do students learn to write on social work programmes?*
2. *What are the most beneficial ways of teaching social work writing?*

Research findings should address each of the research questions at attempt to answer them.

Hypothesis

A hypothesis is an untested idea or proposition which research can test out. A hypothesis may arise from the research questions or be developed in order to help answer them. Not all research is based on a hypothesis.

An example of a hypothesis associated with the research questions suggested above would be:

Social work students learn writing most effectively when assessments combine academic and practice skills.

Research findings may prove or disprove a hypothesis.

Literature review

The purpose of a literature review is to provide a 'state of the art' or précis of current knowledge in the field of study that is being investigated. It is the starting point for any research and provides both the context and justification for a new investigation. A literature review should identify the 'gap' in the literature which the research will attempt to address. A literature review is by its nature selective in that it draws together the existing published work which is most relevant to the research questions and hypothesis posed.

Data

Data is the word used for the information collected while undertaking research, for example responses to questionnaires from participants or statistical figures based on observations, tests or experiments. The kind of data collected and the way in which it is collected rely on the methodology.

Methodology

The methodology used by a research project refers to the way in which the investigation is carried out. In its simplest terms it describes and justifies the way in which data is collected but the methodology is also underpinned by the theoretical approach taken by the researcher which is based upon more complex, philosophical ideas about the nature of knowledge. You may come across the term 'epistemology' which means the theory of knowledge which informs the methods through which it is created. There are two well established approaches to research methodologies, quantitative and qualitative. Quantitative research, traditionally associated with the natural sciences, is broadly concerned with data that can be counted and measured and findings that can be replicated in such a ways that they can be reliably applied to other contexts (Solomon and Draine, 2010). You may have come across the term 'positivist' to describe quantitative approaches, which means the belief that knowledge can be verified and proved. Qualitative, or interpretive, methodologies are more usually associated with human and social sciences. They focus less on measurable or replicable data drawn from, for example, human experience or behaviour. In reality the distinction between qualitative and quantitative is not always this clear and 'mixed-methods' methodologies draw on both approaches to data collection.

Analysis

Once data has been collected it is analysed by researchers in order to draw conclusions based on the original research questions. The way in which analysis is undertaken is strongly influenced by the methodology and the researcher's epistemological approach to creating and using new knowledge.

Findings

The findings draw together the outcome of the analysis and address the original research questions and hypothesis, if one was identified.

As suggested above, the ways in which each of these elements are used depends on the kind of research that is being undertaken. The following case studies illustrate some of the forms of research you might encounter in your studies.

You will encounter a wide range of activities which might be referred to as 'research' and not all will include all of these elements. Some will involve more systematic processes than others and not all will generate 'new' knowledge. You may come across the term **empirical research**, which means that the research is based on original data, rather than conclusions being drawn from theorising on previously **secondary research**, in other words research that has already been published elsewhere. The following short case studies illustrate some of the kinds of research social workers, including social work students and educators, might be involved in:

Case Study

Gilli's assignment research

Gilli is a social work student and has an essay for her social work law module. She is asked to undertake research into the development of legislation relating to the protection and safeguarding of children for an assessed group presentation. This activity involves a selective review and analysis of existing literature relevant to the task, but would not generate new or original knowledge.

Liam's dissertation research

Liam is studying for a master's and as part of his qualification he needs to undertake a small research project. He chooses to undertake desktop research into the ways in which people with dementia are portrayed in the media. This activity involves a systematic analysis of relevant existing literature and requires research questions, a clear methodology and analysis of data collected but would not necessarily generate new or original knowledge.

Arun's practice research

Arun is a social work team leader and is involved in a two-year research project with researchers from the local university. The research is internally funded (by the university and local authority) and aims to explore the experiences of young people leaving the looked-after system. The research involves young people as co-researchers and gathers data though interviews, focus groups and collaborative expressive performance. This activity involves a systematic analysis of existing literature and requires research questions, a clear methodology, analysis of the data and reporting of findings. It would be expected to generate original knowledge.

Joseph's research

Joseph is a social work academic and researcher who has published widely on social housing and poverty. He is currently leading a team of researchers from five universities on an externally funded project which is modelling the impact of changes in the system of provision of social housing across the country. The study involves collecting statistical data from each region and measuring changes in expenditure, service provision and correlation with a range of data which measure poverty and social exclusion.

This activity involves a systematic analysis of existing literature and requires research questions, a clear methodology, rigorous analysis of the data and public reporting of findings. It would be expected to generate original knowledge.

These case studies illustrate the range of research that you may be involved in or use as part of your studies.

Activity 6.1

You can read examples of published research in academic and professional journals. Search for one of the following journals and browse for any articles that interest you. For each one try and find each of the elements listed described above (research questions, hypotheses, literature review, data, methodology, analysis and findings). You should be able to access online journals through your university library, but research is increasingly being made available online without a paid subscription. You can find Open Access articles through websites such as the Directory of Open Access Journals which can be found at https://doaj.org/.

- *Social Work Education* (Open Access)
- *British Journal of Social Work*
- *Community Care*
- *Critical Social Work* (Open Access)
- *Journal of Social Work*
- *Journal of Social Work Education*
- *Journal of Comparative Social Work* (Open Access)
- *Social Work Research*
- *Critical Social Work* (Open Access)
- *International Social Work*

Don't worry if you found some of these articles quite challenging to read. As you get more practice in reading research articles you will become more familiar with the format and vocabulary used. You will also become practised at how to get a quick overview of an article. A good way to do this is to read the abstract (a short precis at the beginning of most articles), discussion and conclusion. You can read the remainder of the article in more detail once you are confident that it is relevant to your topic of interest.

Using research evidence in your studies

In Chapter 3 you have already been introduced to doing your research in preparation for writing academic assignments. Sources for academic assignments can include books, journal articles and reliable websites (see Table 6.1) (see also below for evaluating the reliability of websites). Your assignments provide an opportunity for you to delve a little deeper into a topic, reading material that is particularly relevant to your own academic or practice interests. Much of the reading that you do will be based to some degree on 'research', although some sources will be closer to original empirical studies than others.

Table 6.1 Sources for academic assignments

Journal articles	Many, but not all, journal articles report on original empirical data. Some articles are 'theoretical' which means that they are based on a review or re-interpretation of previously published research. Some journal articles, particularly in social work, are 'case study' or 'practice studies' which means that they may be based on limited original data but reflect on current practice examples.
Professional journals or magazines	These are aimed at professionals in a specific field and although they contain some research-based articles these are more commonly secondary research.
Textbooks	Textbooks vary greatly in terms of the way in which they draw on research. Publishers and authors will determine the readership and purpose when a publishing contract is agreed. Some books will be closely based on original research and aimed at an academic audience, although most research is published first in journal articles. Some books, such as this one, will draw on secondary research and be written for a student audience.
Websites	Original empirical research is rarely published on websites but some do provide a source of valuable secondary research. Great caution is needed when searching for research on websites as they are not subject to the same level of publishing rigour as journal articles and books.

Why is it important for social workers to understand and use research?

You may have already encountered the term 'evidence-based practice' in your studies as it is a concept which underpins much of social work education and practice. Mullen et al. suggest that 'evidence-based practice' (EBP) is grounded in the idea that practitioners should and can base their interventions on the best available evidence rather than on expert opinion, intuition, authority, tradition or common sense (Mullen et al., 2008). I would argue that through the acquisition of knowledge, skills and practice experience applied within a set of professional standards, social workers are in fact 'experts' but their opinion should still be grounded in evidence. Parker suggests that there is a close relationship between reflective practice and becoming a 'like-minded practitioner', which he defines as a practitioner who will 'act, critically analyse and reflect on the rationale for actions . . . to produce an evidence-based understanding' (Parker, 2010, p25).

The professionalisation of social work over the past six decades has established evidence as an essential cornerstone of good practice. Evidence in this context refers mainly to published research which has been peer reviewed. Peer reviewing is the process through which academics and researchers scrutinise new research prior to it being published in order to ensure that the findings have been rigorously produced using a systematic methodology. Social work practice may also be underpinned by evidence from local or national enquiry reports, legislation or published theory which justifies or explains their practice. While evidence-based practice is important, the application of evidence from any source to inform or justify interventions should be undertaken with caution due to the complexity of real-life practice. The application of evidence, or theory, relies on the judgement of the practitioner. Newly qualified practitioners will be less able to draw on their experience informed by prior reading and learning, but even experienced social workers should update their learning and engagement with relevant research, either through individual professional development or training. While the sources of new knowledge may be consciously drawn on, knowledge assimilated over the years can become implicit and less conscious in practice. All sources of knowledge, however, are potentially valuable as explicit evidence in both practice writing (such as assessment or court reports) and also in writing which is assessed. To illustrate the ways in which knowledge and evidence consider the following case study.

Case Study

Raj's assessment of Rosemary

Raj is an experienced social worker in a team which supports adults with learning disabilities. She has been working with Rosemary, a 24-year-old with Down's syndrome, for six months and she is now due for a final assessment before her EHC Plan comes to an end. Rosemary finished a training course at her local college last month and so plans are needed to support her in getting employment. A new issue has arisen, however, as Rosemary has requested to move from the family home to supported community accommodation. One of the reasons for this request is that Rosemary has become sexually active and this is a cause of anxiety for her parents and potentially raises a safeguarding issue. Rosemary's parents are not aware of her request, but in previous contact with Raj have expressed high levels of anxiety about their daughter's expressed wish to have intimate relationships, which they feel would put her at risk emotionally and that if she were to become pregnant she would not have the capacity to care for a child safely. Rosemary's parents are also anxious about what she will do now that she has completed her college course. There had been plans for her to begin work experience arranged by the college but this fell through and she is now at home all day and, according to her parents, getting bored and depressed.

Comment

Raj's assessment will be informed by her discussions with Rosemary, Rosemary's parents and also input from her college tutor and GP. In addition to this information provided by people with first-hand knowledge about Rosemary, Raj will draw on research. In this context research refers to knowledge that she will apply to her analysis of the situation drawn from reliable sources. Some of this knowledge will already be familiar to Raj as she learnt it during her training or in the course of her job and she uses it regularly. Raj may also need to consult new or less familiar research, either to update her knowledge or ensure there have been no changes. Table 6.2 illustrates the sources which Raj drew on in her research – you might like to follow some of these to update your own knowledge.

(Continued)

(Continued)

Table 6.2 Sources of Raj's research

Legislation	Policy/statutory guidance	Textbooks	Web resources	Journal articles
Care Act 2014	Special educational needs and disability code of practice: 0 to 25 years	Kingsley, EP and Walker-Hirsch, L (2007) 'A parent's perspective: supporting challenges and strategies', in L Walker-Hirsch (ed.) *The Facts of Life and More … Sexuality and Intimacy for People with Intellectual Disabilities*. Baltimore, MD: Paul H Brookes, pp75–93.	Transition into adult services https://www.mencap.org.uk/advice-and-support/children-and-young-people/education-support/transition-adult-services	Blamires, K (2015) A summary of government initiatives relating to employment for people with learning disabilities in England. *Tizard Learning Disability Review*, 20 (3), pp151–165.
Carers UK (2014)	Education and health care plan	Heslop, P and Hebron, C (eds) (2020) *Promoting the Health and Well-Being of People with Learning Disabilities*. Springer.	Mencap (2019) *What Is a Learning Disability?* www.mencap.org.uk	Hemm, C, Dagnan, D and Meyer, TD (2018) Social anxiety and parental overprotection in young adults with and without intellectual disabilities, *Journal of Applied Research in Intellectual Disabilities* (JARID), 31 (3), pp360–368.
Children and Families Act 2014	Department of Health (2001) *Valuing People: A New Strategy for Learning Disability for the 21st Century*, Cm 5086.	Ledger, S, Townson, L with Docherty, D (2014) *Sexuality and Relationships in the Lives of People with Intellectual Disabilities: Standing in My Shoes*. Jessica Kingsley.	The National Institute for Health and Care Excellence (NICE) (2016) Overarching principles, in *Transition from Children's to Adults' Services for Young People Using Health or Social Care Services*. www.nice.org.uk The National Institute for Health and Care Excellence (NICE) (2016) *Transition from Children's to Adults' Services for Young People Using Health or Social Care Services*. https://www.nice.org.uk NHS (2019) *Assessing Capacity*. www.nhs.uk Towers, C (2013) *Thinking Ahead: A Planning Guide for Families*. London: Foundation for People with Learning Disabilities. www.mentalhealth.org.uk	Downs, C and Craft, A (1996) Sexuality and profound and multiple impairment, *Tizard Learning Disability Review*, 1 (4). pp17–22. McCarthy, M (1998) Whose body is it anyway? Pressures and control for women with learning disabilities. *Disability and Society*, 13 (4), pp557–574.

The examples here only relate to knowledge that is specific to Rosemary's needs and circumstances. Raj would also have drawn on a wide range of other theory, legislation and policy applicable to social work practice more generally, for example knowledge relating to communication, values and social work methods. In daily practice social workers will rarely have time to read sources such as these to inform their practice with an individual service user. As part of your professional registration, however, you are required to maintain and develop your knowledge through qualification and beyond. The Social Work England Professional Standards refer to keeping up to date and using knowledge in a number of places, but these are some of the key relevant standards:

3.2 Use information from a range of appropriate sources, including supervision, to inform assessments, to analyse risk, and to make a professional decision.
3.5 Hold different explanations in mind and use evidence to inform my decisions.
4.3 Keep my practice up to date and record how I use research, theories and frameworks to inform my practice and my professional judgement.
4.4 Demonstrate good subject knowledge on key aspects of social work practice and develop knowledge of current issues in society and social policies impacting on social work.

(Social Work England, 2019)

Activity 6.2

Think of someone you have worked with, ideally someone you have completed an assessment for. This could be someone you are working with now or have worked with in the past. Using a copy of Table 6.2, list the sources of research that you used or could use. Include in your list a note of knowledge that you already have and also new research that you need to undertake to update, refresh or develop new knowledge to apply to your practice. Keep your list as you will need it again in the next activity.

Evaluating online resources using PROMPT

You may have noticed in Table 6.2 and perhaps in your own list of sources that there are a good number that are available online. There are rigorous quality controls for material published in books and in academic journals but these do not apply to resources online. This means that while you can generally trust material accessed from published sources (such as books or journals even when they are available online) care is needed to verify the reliability of material accessed on websites. There are some websites that you can be confident contain reliable information and some of these are identifiable by the end of the URL. For example any websites with a URL ending in .gov.uk will be UK national or local government websites and any websites ending with .ac.uk will be UK academic institutions. Both of these sources should be reliable, but it is always wise to question any source and you are likely to want to access websites other than just academic or government sources. The Open University has developed the mnemonic PROMPT (Open University, 2014) to help students to evaluate online sources, and this can apply equally well when researching information in practice (see Table 6.3).

Table 6.3 Using PROMPT

Presentation	Is the information presented and communicated clearly?
	Consider the language, layout and structure.
Relevance	Is the content relevant to the topic you are researching?
	Look at the introduction or overview to find out what it is mainly about.
Objectivity	Is the content biased or motivated by a particular agenda?
	Is the language emotive?
	Are there hidden, vested interests?
Method	Is it clear how the data/content were collected?
	Were the methods appropriate and can you trust them?
Provenance	Is it clear where the information has come from?
	Can you identify the author(s)/organisation(s), and are they trustworthy?
	Are there references/citations that lead to further reading and are they trustworthy sources?
Timeliness	How up-to-date is the material? Is it clear when it was written?
	Does the date of writing meet your requirements, or would it be obsolete?

(Adapted from Open University, 2014)

Activity 6.3

Return to your list of sources from Activity 6.2 and review any that are from online sources using the PROMPT criteria.

1. Were there any web pages which you think on reflection may not be reliable sources?
2. Can you find the publication date?
3. Is the information provided referenced and how convinced are you about the reliability of the data or research on which it is based?
4. Can you see who owns or publishes the website and, if so, do you think they may have any commercial, political or ethical bias?

If you are struggling to find a publication date, this can often be found at the bottom of the webpage. You can sometimes also find a copyright mark here too which indicates who is responsible for the content. You should also check whether the webpage you are using appears at the top of a search with 'Ad' next to the title, which indicates that the search engine provider has been paid to list this webpage towards the top of the search list. This does not necessarily suggest that the site is not reliable but it should be treated with caution.

Using PROMPT is a useful way to check the reliability of your sources whether you are using research for an academic assignment or to inform your practice. You will develop your skills in identifying reliable sources with practice and also get to know the useful and reliable sources for your own needs. Your ability to critically appraise research presented in any source will also develop with practice, but one useful way to develop your skills is to undertake your own research. You may need to do this as part of your qualifying programme, particularly if you are undertaking a masters course, but you may also have the opportunity to undertake research as part of your role as a qualified social worker.

Undertaking your own research

The ways in which you might become involved in research can range from taking a systematic, evidence-based approach to your practice – in other words as a research-minded practitioner as defined by Parker (2010) – through to undertaking or participating in empirical research. It is beyond the scope of this chapter to explore how to undertake your own research in any depth but this final section of the chapter explores writing up when you undertake your own research, either as part of your academic studies or in practice.

Writing up research as part of your studies

It is common for students to undertake small-scale research projects as part of their studies, particularly at master's level. More extensive research is required if you undertake a higher degree such as a professional doctorate or a PhD. Social workers at any of these levels will often focus their research on an aspect of practice, which brings its own specific challenges as discussed below.

At the undergraduate and master's level writing up this research can involve you in writing an extended length assignment which can be significantly more challenging than writing a standard assignment. This might be referred to as a dissertation, research assignment or extended practice study and the specific requirements and length will depend on the programme you are studying. At the level of a doctorate the final piece of written work is called a thesis and is normally in the range of 80,000 to 100,000 words. Regardless of the level of study or length of the writing to be submitted there are some principles which should guide your writing about research. These are outlined using CAPS (see Table 6.4).

Table 6.4 CAPS principles

Context	The context of a research-based assignment completed as part of a programme of study is the university. However, in social work programmes it is common for research to involve practice contexts such as agencies, service users and fellow professionals. This adds a dimension which requires students to take particular care over issues such as ethics and confidentiality. It is also important to be aware that all assignments that are completed as part of a qualifying programme (a programme leading to professional qualification) may have a bearing on judgements about your professional competence, even when it is not your practice that is being assessed. It is possible, for example, that serious breaches of confidentiality or academic misconduct could be considered as reasons to question a student's suitability for professional qualification and consequent registration.

(Continued)

Table 6.4 (Continued)

Audience	The primary audience, as with any academic assignment, is the lecturer or tutor who will be assessing your work. The expectations of your assessor will vary depending on your level of study and these expectations should be grounded in the assessment criteria. Research assignments will often provide an opportunity for you to explore at a greater level of detail than most assignments. At the undergraduate level this can mean that assessors are reading assignments about topics in which you have greater expertise than your reader, and so it is important not to make assumptions about concepts or practice contexts that you refer to.
Purpose	The purpose of a research assignment is to test your ability to undertake and report on a systematic inquiry. This inquiry may be into existing research (conducting a literature review or theoretical paper), it may be an inquiry into practice or it might involve original empirical research. Regardless of the nature of the inquiry the assessors will be judging whether you have demonstrated a systematic approach to your data collection and analysis. In the context of social work in particular assessors will also expect you to demonstrate that you have respected confidentiality and followed appropriate ethical approvals and codes of practice.
Self	The concept of self in any research study can be complex, but this is particularly so in social work. Traditionally researchers strive to be objective, impartial observers, taking an 'emic' stance as outsiders to the topic there are researching. Research undertaken in social work, particularly where this is related to your own practice context, results in you having conflicting and overlapping roles as participants and researchers, sometimes referred to in ethnographic research as an 'etic' stance. Where you are involved in any way in the context you are investigating, it is very important to recognise this overtly and consider the impact of being an 'insider' might have on your relationship with participants and to the ways in which you analyse your data.

Activity 6.4

This section has considered writing up research as an academic assignment. CAPS is equally applicable to writing up research undertaken within the context of practice as a qualified worker. If you have been involved in this kind of research, even as a participant rather than a researcher, use this as an example and try to complete a CAPS analysis for this project. If you do not have an example or experience to draw on, look back at the mini case studies of either Arun or Joseph and use these to complete the activity.

Chapter summary

This chapter has introduced you to the essential elements of a research report for most purposes. As you have seen throughout this book, however, the specific requirements of texts vary depending on the context. Whether you are writing up your own research or not, you will be required to use and evaluate research on your social work course and also possibly as a practitioner. This chapter should provide you with a starting point to think critically about how to share the findings of your own research convincingly, and also critically evaluate the research you read about.

Further reading

Carey, M (2012) *Qualitative Research Skills for Social Work: Theory and Practice.* Burlington, VT: Ashgate.

This is a useful book if you are considering undertaking a research project. It provides a straightforward outline for planning a qualitative research study with a particular focus on social work. There is a useful section on writing up your project.

Carey, M (2013) *The Social Work Dissertation.* London: McGraw-Hill.

This book focuses on the research process overall but does include writing up your research. It is specific to social work and is of relevance both during training and when conducting research post qualifying.

Clark, T and Bryman, A (2019) *How to Do Your Social Research Project or Dissertation.* Oxford: Oxford University Press.

While this is not specifically about social work research, the discussion is very relevant and the book provides a clear outline of planning, undertaking and writing up a research project.

Part Two

Writing in social work practice

7

Case recording

Lucy Rai and Theresa Lillis

Introduction

In this chapter you will learn about case recording and its importance as a practice tool in social work. The chapter will explore the legal and regulatory function of case recording and the ways in which the institutional context has an impact on how recording is undertaken. You will again apply CAPS to aid reflection on case recording in your own practice context, but you will also explore some genuine examples of case recording from the research data gathered by the Writing in Social Work Practice project. Through these examples you will learn about some of the elements of case recording, what makes them effective and also some of the challenges involved. Finally you will consider how different voices can be expressed through your case recording, including your own professional voice and those of service users and carers.

What is the purpose of case recording?

A comment frequently made by social workers is that 'If it's not written down it didn't happen' (Lillis et al., 2017). While this might sound like an exaggeration, writing is central to social work practice and at the heart of such writing is case recording. In simple terms case recording is the documentation of social work intervention with a specific service user. It is variously referred to as 'recording', 'case notes' or 'record keeping'. In current practice case recording is normally digital, in other words it is written and saved on an ICT system. Records are generally written directly by the social worker responsible for the 'case' or specific service user. Where a social worker is involved with a family, there will be a 'case file' on each individual, although there may be some duplication of information across family members. Case recording is therefore important in its own right, ensuring that a fair and accurate record of events, situations and concerns is kept. Case notes are also used as a key source of information in many other kinds of written texts, such as assessment reports, court reports and requests for services.

There are several purposes of case recording. Drawing on the suggest purposes identified by the Social Care Institute for Excellence (SCIE), recording can be broadly divided as 'supporting practice' and 'regulatory duties':

Supporting practice:

1.   It supports good care and support.
2.   It promotes continuity of care and communication with other agencies.
3.   It is a tool to help identify themes and challenges in a person's life.

Regulatory duty:

1.   It is a legal requirement and part of staff's professional duty.
2.   It is evidence – for court, complaints and investigations.
3.   It is key to accountability – to people who use services, to managers, to inspections and audits.

Adapted from SCIE (2020).

Supporting practice

Maintaining clear and accurate records is a requirement within the professional standards that govern the practice of all social workers across the nations of the UK (Social Work England, 2019; Social Care Wales, 2019; Scottish Social Services Council, 2016; Northern Ireland Social Care Council, 2019). At a fundamental level of supporting practice, recording is the way in which basic information about someone receiving support or intervention from a social worker can be identified – this data would include name, date of birth, address and contact details. Case recording, however, is far more than contact information. As indicated by SCIE (2020), recording is a planning and assessment tool which is intended to ensure that effective services are provided, which involves compiling often highly complex information from multiple sources.

There are numerous ways in which recording supports day-to-day practice but in essence, when it is used effectively, case recoding is an important tool for social workers and colleagues from other professions:

*   to gather, co-ordinate and synthesise information from multiple sources
*   to create chronologies

- to identify themes and patterns to inform practice
- to undertake and record assessments and reviews
- to provide professional recommendations on action and service provision
- to share information across services and between workers within an agency.

Case recording is therefore much more than factual information and although a professional responsibility and a legal duty, it is also a sophisticated tool which facilitates practice, particularly where information needs to be shared or co-ordinated between social workers, across different service users and to ensure effective multi-agency working.

As with all practice, case recording should meet the values enshrined in the relevant professional standards, which in England are set by Social Work England (Social Work England, 2019). Case recording is just one example of the ways in which the power of social work practice needs to be used with great caution. Evidence from case notes can be used as evidence to make life-changing decisions about people's lives and so it is particularly important that they promote confidentiality, social justice, human rights and partnership working and challenge injustice and discrimination. The application of these values will be referred to throughout this chapter but are particularly relevant through representing the voices of service users and case notes are accurate and based on evidence and informed professional judgement.

Regulatory duty

Recording is governed by legal requirements which apply to social workers employed within a statutory setting as well as private and third-sector agencies. Legislation governs how recording should be kept and stored as well as access to files for service users, discussed below. Recording is also a procedural requirement. Social work is a profession which carries statutory duties and requires significant public trust, and this accountability to the public is in part evidenced through accurate and timely recording. Public accountability is particularly important in social work due to the sensitivity of the work, which is primarily undertaken in the context of the care and protection of vulnerable people. In addition to the trusted role of social work in providing care and protective services, the profession is largely resourced through government funding and this is also a reason for the activities of the profession coming under close scrutiny. Written records provide a tool for the actions of social work to be scrutinised to ensure that agencies and individual workers are adhering to professional standards and codes of practice, to meeting agency standards as required by bodies such as the Quality Care Commission and OFSTED (in England), the Care Inspectorate (Scotland), the Care Inspectorate Wales (Wales) and the Regulation and Quality Improvement Agency (Northern Ireland).

The institutional context

The effectiveness of case recording of course does not rely only on the writing of social workers. Requirements and systems for recording are established and monitored at an agency and sometimes national level, often leaving little discretion for individual social workers. Moreover, 'effectiveness' is potentially misleading as it implies that there is an uncontentious 'purpose' of recording. In reality there are tensions between the require-ment for recording to be a tool for audit and accountability on the one hand and supporting practice on the other. The tensions between effective practice and institu-tional accountability is well illustrated by the failure of a national IT database (the Integrated Children's System or ICS) in the early 2000s. The ICS was introduced follow-ing Lord Laming's report into the death of Victoria Climbié and was intended to improve the co-ordination of information-sharing in children's services (Seymour and Seymour, 2011). Within a couple of years Unison called for the withdrawal of the ICS, a call strengthened by the findings of the inquiry into the death of 'Baby P' in 2008. This report suggested that the system was *undermining safe professional practice and increasing risk.* Failings identified within the system included its overemphasis on data entry, top-down micro-management and scrutiny, all of which inhibited professional discretion and the flexibility required in frontline practice (White et al., 2010). In a review of the impact of the ICS, Wastell and White suggested that records had become *primarily ways of achiev-ing accountability, providing an electronic audit trail showing that correct procedures have been followed. This privileging has subordinated a crucial part of the professional sense-making process, namely reading and understanding complex cases, unfolding across time and space* (Wastell and White, 2009, p144).

As a result of concerns raised, a key recommendation of the Social Work Task Force (DoH, 2009) was to reform the data management system. Recording systems for children's services, along with all service user groups, have subsequently been localised and agencies have had more involvement in their design to ensure that they better support professional practice. Over the past decade a range of software systems has been developed which, while not without difficulties, have been designed for social work across all domains (children's, adults, mental health) and allow individual authorities and services to select the provider which best meets their need. Community Care undertook an audit of providers in 2019 which illustrates the range of packages being used across adult and children's services.

Table 7.1 Providers across adult and children's services

	Children's	Adults
LiquidLogic	44%	34%
Mosaic (Servelec)	24%	26%
CareFirst (OLM)	8%	14%
Frameworki (Servelec)	6%	6%
CareDirector	3%	3%
Swift (OLM)	3%	7%
Other	12%	10%

Source: Community Care (2019).

In this study 60 per cent of social workers consulted still reported frustrating difficul-ties with the software (Community Care, 2019), indicating that moving away from the initial ICT systems, such as the ICS, has not entirely resolved the challenges of digital recording. Nevertheless, social workers are required to record via the ICT system selected by their authority and IT specialists within each authority are constantly seeking to improve the systems.

What do case notes look like?

A recent research project, Writing in Professional Social Work Practice or WiSP (see for example, Lillis et al 2017; Leedham et al 2020; Lillis et al 2020), investigating the routine writing of social workers highlighted case notes as one of four key types of writing central to all social work practice. The other three are reports (which you will explore in Chapter 8) and also emails and handwritten notes. The key characteristics of case notes as identified in the WiSP study are set out in Table 7.2. Not surprisingly, there is also considerable variation, as social workers have to record many different kinds of situations, people and needs. Some of these variations are outlined in Table 7.3.

Table 7.2 Typical case notes shared the following features (after Lillis et al 2017; 36–7)

Audience	No explicit audience (except where emails are copied in as case notes) but the agency is the implied audience
Design	• Part of IT system • Select type of case note from drop down menu • Typically blank text box (some systems have *Analysis* subhead)
Agency function	To record all actions, events, interactions and correspondence relating to a specific individual
Medium	Digital-IT system
Typical elements	• Description of what happened or what was said that gave rise to the case recording, for example a phone call or series of calls, voicemails received, unanswered phone calls, home visits made, critical incidents, paperwork submitted or uploaded on IT system • Description of action, for example what has been done or is planned to do and by whom, often stating name, role, contact details. Also decisions, events, incidents, interaction, arrangements and agreements made • Evaluation, sometimes interspersed and/or at end of case notes • Emails and SMS are also often copied into case notes

Table 7.3 Case notes varied in the following ways

Length	Ranged between 6 and 1,996 words
Self	Varied in terms of how the social worker is presented and how others are presented. For example, sometimes direct speech is used – he said 'I don't want to...'
Style	A range of stylistic features used such as bulleted/numbered list, full/abbreviated sentences, paragraphs/continuous text, social workers own headings/templated headings (e.g. for statutory visit case notes), unexplained acronyms
Explicit evaluation and analysis	In some cases the social worker includes explicit evaluation, for example 'I think that...', 'It is clear that...', 'My recommendation is that...'
Contextualising of case	In some cases records referred to previous events and the history of the case while others foregrounded the present

The consistent or typical features of case notes arise largely from the statutory function of such notes and requirements arising from inquiry reports, such as the development of IT systems which facilitate inter-agency communication. Despite this, variations arise both between and within agencies or service user group providers. These can be to do with agency policies, the practices of individual social workers or teams and also the requirements of particular service user groups or cases. Some variations will also arise from unintentional inconsistencies.

Why are case notes challenging?

All social workers in the WiSP study emphasised the importance of keeping high-quality up-to-date case notes but they also pointed to some challenges, two key ones being time and interruptions. In a busy working day, social workers reported having insufficient time to spend on writing case notes and that they were frequently interrupted by phone calls and discussions of specific cases with colleagues and managers. This means that a key aspect of professional practice is learning how to write case notes quickly, and this takes considerable practice so do not expect to be able to do this immediately. It also means that your case notes will not always be written in full sentences. Social workers use bullet points, abbreviations and subheadings and these are all useful strategies for recording important information quickly.

While inquiries, case reviews and research have identified that there are concerns and challenges associated with case recording, the degree of scrutiny of this aspect of professional social work writing also indicates its importance. As you saw above case recording has multiple important functions including accountability and support for practice. As such it is not only a tool to *record* practice but also a tool *for* practice, in other words it is through recording that analysis takes place, assessments are drawn and decisions are guided. Assessments and decision-making in social work frequently draw on historical and chronological accounts of events, piecing together a jigsaw and balancing risks and protective factors in order to reach recommendations. The information required for this lies within case recording and as such it is an invaluable practice tool when used effectively, for example through the creation and use of chronologies to inform assessments (Turney et al., 2011).

What makes an effective case record?

Case records should primarily communicate information clearly to the reader. This can be challenging for a number of reasons as discussed above. CAPS can be a useful starting place to reflect on some of these challenges. The illustration in Table 7.4 is very general but is followed by an example based on case recording for a specific service user.

Completing a very general application of CAPS as illustrated in Table 7.5 can be a useful exercise if you are new to an agency or service user group. It can, for example, prompt you to find out which case management system is used and whether you are familiar with it. (There is a further discussion of case management systems below.) It can also prompt you to make sure you have sought out and accessed any agency-specific policies on recording. Once completed at this general level, future applications of CAPS will be more useful at the level of specific service users or case records. You will not have time or need to apply CAPS every time you undertake a written task, but this can be a useful exercise as part of your training, professional development or supervision.

Table 7.4 CAPS example

		Ask yourself...	Illustrative answer
C	Context	Are there any specific requirements arising from the agency or service user group that I am recording for? Is there anything I need to be aware of about the case management system (software for recording) used in my agency? Are there policies around timescales for completing or signing off the recording?	I am working in a statutory adult services team in Blankshire, which uses Mosaic as its case management system. Mosaic allows access to integrated health and social care records. There are local policies on recording which I can refer to online. The policy requires that all recording should be completed within three working days unless a different timescale is indicated by a specific endorsed procedure and that service users should be made aware of their right to see their file and given the opportunity to correct any errors or omissions and add any disagreements.
A	Audience	Who is the recording primarily written for? Who else may read all or extracts from the record?	The people who need to read this case recording include members of the adult services team including my line manager and the service user. Extracts from the case recording may also be used to complete other documents such as reports or financial assessments.
P	Purpose	Why is the information being recorded?	The recording is a statutory and professional requirement in order to document intervention and also any service user needs and risks.
S	Self	Who am I writing this record? Which aspects of my identity are relevant?	I am writing as a qualified social worker who is also an accountable representative of my agency. As such I should draw on my professional knowledge and skills and also adhere to the statutory and policy requirements of my agency.

Table 7.5 Case recording using CAPS

		Ask yourself...	Illustrative answer
C	Context	Is there information about the specific service user that I need to keep in mind, such as ongoing risks/assessments/ reviews of services? Are there related files or existing and known communication issues? Are there other agencies involved with records that need to be consulted or shared?	Mr X is a new referral but he has an existing file as he was the subject of an adult safeguarding assessment two years ago. He has been living independently since that time with support from third-sector services which he pays for himself. There is no other family involvement or support. Mr X has no impairments which affect his ability to read his files. Relevant information on Mr X is held by his GP, the hospital and the day centre which he attends, which is run by a third-sector organisation.

(Continued)

Table 7.5 (Continued)

		Ask yourself...	Illustrative answer
A	Audience	Who is the recording primarily written for? Who else may read all or extracts from the record?	My colleagues in the adult services team, which includes review officers, occupational therapists and my line manager. Mr X will also be able to read the recording and will be provided with an opportunity to amend/add information. Extracts from the case recording are likely to be used to complete my assessment reports and any financial assessment which arises from it.
P	Purpose	Why is the information being recorded?	Mr X has been referred due to new adult safeguarding concerns and the recording is both a statutory requirement and an important tool for planning my intervention. My agency/line manager will be able to use the recording to make sure that timescales for assessment and the provision of any services/interventions are kept to. If I become unavailable the recording will also enable one of my colleagues to pick up and continue the work with Mr X. The recording also facilitates multi-agency working, particularly with colleagues in health who have access to the integrated case management system.
S	Self	Who am I writing this record as? Which aspects of my identity are relevant?	I am writing as a qualified social worker who is also an accountable representative of my agency. As such I should draw on my professional knowledge and skills and also adhere to the statutory and policy requirements of my agency. However, my agency requires that case recording is written in the voice of the service user, so I am also writing as or on behalf of Mr X

The example given in Table 7.5 is for a relatively straightforward example as there are a limited number of *current* audiences, although the historical use of case recording means that the audience could be wider if these records became relevant again, for example if a service user asks to see their records or as evidence for court or safeguarding assessments. Considerations for the 'Self' section are challenging where, as in this example, there is an expectation to write in the service user's voice. This can be a significant challenge both linguistically and in trying to include both the service user's voice and your own professional voice. This involves careful weaving and articulation of facts, opinions and professional judgements.

Activity 7.1

Copy the table above and try to complete one for your agency and one for a specific service user you are working with. Think about how the case recording you are required to do differs from the examples above. Can you identify why any variations might be justified?

Practice examples of case recording

In the final section of this chapter you will reflect on two short case studies, one from children's services and one from adult services. Both draw on authentic data gathered by the WiSP research project (http://www.writinginsocialwork.com/).

Activity 7.2

For each of the following case studies, read the outline and extracts from case records and then reflect on the following questions:

1. Do you think each case note clearly describes a particular event, contact, situation?
2. Why do you think the social worker included a note on an attempted visit in the second case study?
3. How clear and explicit do you think the case notes are? Can you identify any of the issues from the SCIE report discussed above?
4. Can you find any examples of the case notes including information provided by other professionals or family members/carer? Is it always clear where information came from?
5. Can you see any examples of either social worker making a recommendation or detailing actions needed?

Children's services example: Sophie

Case Study (Extracts have been fully anonymised to remove all identifying information)

Sophie is a 14-year-old girl attending mainstream school. The allocated social worker was concerned about her drug misuse, her socialising with older men and her being potentially at risk of child sexual exploitation (CSE). Working with Sophie over a period of four months involved the writing of many case notes as well as other documents. All of these feed into formal assessment reports (which you will read more about in Chapter 8).

Extracts from case notes

> **Extract 1**
>
> **T/C FROM School [drop down menu in ICT system for classifying what case note based on e.g. t/c, home visit etc.]**
>
> Sophie is reported to look as though she has taken drugs. She has wide pupils and is not in lesson

(Continued)

(Continued)

Extract 2

T/C FROM School [drop down menu in ICT system for classifying what case note based on e.g. t/c, home visit etc.]

Member of staff has overhead her saying she is going to Summer Park to pick some pills up to give them to Nick. Sophie reported to school that yesterday her mouth was bleeding and today nose bleeding. Sophie has been sent home this morning. Her behaviour has deteriorated.

Extract 3

Home visit [drop down menu in ICT system for classifying what case note based on e.g. t/c, home visit etc.]

Sophie's mother stated that Sophie has been coming home earlier and staying in watching films with her. S's mother stated there has been no recent mentions of Sam. S's mother has asked Sophie not to hang around with Amy as she is too old.

S's mother stated that things have been much better with Sophie. S's mother attempted to wake Sophie up. This took about 15 minutes. I asked if I could go upstairs and talk to Sophie.

Sophie was in bed and did not want to talk with me at first. Then when I was with Sophie she was happy to talk. I spoke with Sophie in her room.

Questioned Sophie on Alan. She stated; they aren't friends, he's weird and tries to hang around with her but she doesn't like him, he walks up to the different groups in town and keeps trying to hang around with them all, there are two main groups (Sophie's group and an older group which Amy is in).

Sophie said it was a girl named Dawn who introduce Alan to her and she knows Dawn from when she went to Highbank school; Dawn lives close to Sophie and their families are friends.

Sophie is not hanging round with Amy now her mum doesn't want her to, but she is still talking to her to say hello.

Adult services example: David

Case study (Extracts have been fully anonymised to remove all identifying information)

David, is an elderly man with dementia who was living with his wife Lucy his main carer. Lucy had recently struggled to care for David given the worsening of his dementia symptoms. The social worker has been working with David and Lucy to assess his needs and to organise temporary respite care for David as well as considering long-term options.

Extract 1

T/C to family member [drop down menu in ICT system for classifying what case note based on e.g. t/c, home visit etc.]

Attempted contact with Lucy (David's wife) re visit. No answer.

Extract 2

Home visit [drop down menu in ICT system for classifying what case note based on e.g. t/c, home visit etc.]

I visited Lucy at home.

I enquired how she was and she stated that she is just coming to terms with everything that has happened. Lucy stated that she hasn't been to visit David yet at the home and is unsure how he is. I stated that I have spoken with the home and they have reported that David has settled ok and is eating well. Lucy stated that she has been told that he keeps looking for his coat. She stated this will be because he wants to leave to go back to Longtown. Lucy stated that he does this when he is at home as he doesn't want to be at Tower Flats. She stated that she tries to stop him but he has been found on other floors at Tower Flats when he is trying to leave.

Lucy stated that she cannot have David back at home. I confirmed that one of my reasons for visiting was to ask her her views for the future. Lucy stated that she can't as she is frightened. I confirmed whether she means she is frightened of David and she confirmed this to be the case. Lucy stated that David is regularly up during the night. She stated that he has been attempting to have sex with her and she cannot have that. She also stated that more recently he has been aggressive with her and has put his fist up to her.

Lucy stated that she is not sure how David's son will feel about this. She asked 'do you think that they will think I am awful for not having him back'. I advised that I have spoken with David's son and he was open to the possibility of David remaining in residential care. I advised Lucy that she has to be honest how she feels as David could only return home if she is able and willing to care for him. Lucy again confirmed that she isn't.

I confirmed therefore, that after I visit David, I suggest we have a meeting including me, Lucy and David's son to discuss further. Lucy was agreeable to this and was happy for this to take place at their apartment at Tower Flats.

Extract 3

T/C from family member [drop down menu in ICT system for classifying what case note based on e.g. t/c, home visit etc.]

T/C from Jane (daughter in law). Jane confirmed that she has been speaking with my colleague in my absence but wanted to ensure that I was aware that David moved to the Tower Flats last Sunday [01/05/19]. Jane stated that The Birches were happy for David to move without 4 weeks' notice. Jane stated that they had to

(Continued)

(Continued)

> pay The Birches a month in advance and therefore, paid the full cost for this period. I confirmed that I will request the purchase order which can be back dated to his date of move if The Birches were agreeable to waivering the notice period. I stated that The Birches should then refund the money they have paid, less David's contributions and the third party top up amount. Jane confirmed that the third party top up is £150. Agreed that I will send the third party top up agreement to Jane.

Comment

Case notes are often written under considerable time pressures so they are often in abbreviated form, for example the 'I' of social worker may not be missing, as in 'Questioned Sophie on Louis'. You may also notice some basic punctuation 'errors' such as no 's' at the end of 'She has wide pupils and is not in lesson'. This may in some cases make the precise meaning unclear.

The key challenge of case notes is to record all details that may be important to understanding a person, a situation or an event, but it can be difficult to predict exactly which details may prove essential when a note is read in the future. While advice often urges social workers to be 'concise', providing concise, relevant description is a highly complex professional skill so be prepared to spend time learning how to do this effectively.

Case notes are also commonly written assuming that the reader has some existing knowledge about the context or history. For example, the third extract above assumes that the reader will have some background knowledge about payment for different kinds of respite and residential care and the processes around when such payments have to be made. To do otherwise would make each case note time-consuming to read and write, but this does mean that someone new to working with a particular person may need to read back through the history and refer to a chronology if one exists.

The examples of both Sophie and David contain a significant amount of information provided by family members/carers and also from another professional (the school teacher in the first case study).

There are examples in the second case study (David) of the social worker confirming planned actions/next steps, such as suggesting a meeting and sending a third-party top-up agreement. Professional judgement is not explicitly stated in these examples, but it is demonstrated by the information that the social workers select to include in the notes. In particular have a look at examples of where information relating to the level of risk is included: these will inform any assessments that take place and so may be drawn on in other documents such as assessment reports.

Of course case notes are just one important type of document that social workers write as part of ongoing investigations and discussions. In the case of Sophie, Figure 7.1 shows which other key documents the social worker wrote. In the case of David, Figure 7.2 shows which other key texts the social worker wrote. All of these feed into formal assessment reports (which you will read more about in Chapter 8: see Lillis et al. 2017 for details of the other text types in Figure 7.2).

Text work
Children's care – Child at risk of
CSE
Over four month period

| Handwritten | Abduction | Network | Case |
| notes | letters | map | notes |

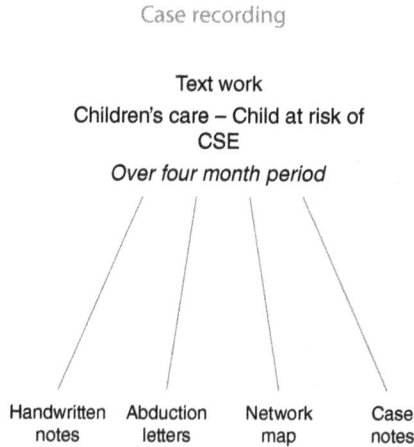

Figure 7.1 Illustrative texts relevant to the 'Sophie' case study

Source: Lillis et al. (2017).

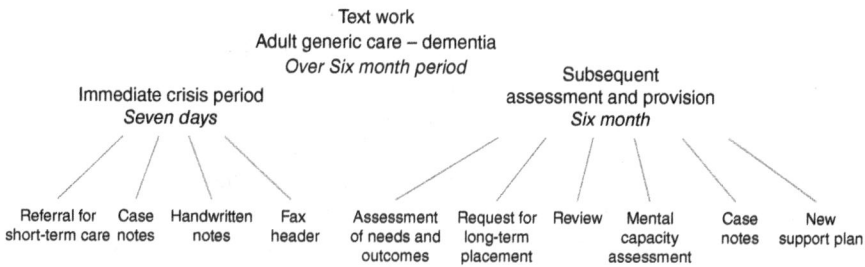

Text work
Adult generic care – dementia
Over Six month period

Immediate crisis period   Subsequent
Seven days   assessment and provision
                                         Six month

Referral for	Case	Handwritten	Fax	Assessment	Request for	Review	Mental	Case	New
short-term care	notes	notes	header	of needs and	long-term		capacity	notes	support plan
				outcomes	placement		assessment		

Figure 7.2 Illustrative texts relevant to the 'David' case study

Source: Lillis et al. (2017).

From these two figures you can see that case notes are just one of many documents that social workers write and that these are often interconnected. The interconnected nature of social work documents means that care is needed to avoid unnecessary duplication but also to ensure that sufficient contextual information is included to enable the intended reader to understand what they are reading. Some documents have a very specific purpose, for example funding applications, and are heavily templated so that there is less discretion for the social workers about what information to include. Other documents, such as the case recording exemplified in this chapter, may have unanticipated purposes and audiences in the future and may require considerably more discretion from the social worker to decide how much detail to include. In the next chapter you will learn about reports (which include assessment, court and review reports) which are perhaps the most challenging and important forms of social work writing as they are the basis for key decisions about people's lives.

Colleagues and service users' access to case recording

Legislation requires that written information is made available to the service user who the record is about on submission of a written request (Data Protection Act 1998). This raises issues about how case notes are written, organised and made available for service users to read. For example, a parent does not have an automatic right to read information about their child, and any request would take into account whether the parent had parental responsibility for the child, whether the parent accessing the files would be in the child's best interest and whether the child has the capacity to give permission. Children considered to have sufficient understanding to make their own requests to read information held about them would be consulted about whether they wanted a parent to read their files. The legislation around access to files means that separate files need to be kept on each child and adult in a family so that if an access request is made one family member will not read information about another member. Where a file does contain information about another person, this content will be 'redacted' or blocked out to preserve the confidentiality of the other person.

Case records may be read not only by service users but also colleagues within and outside of your own agency. For example, in addition to a service user using their legal right to access their files, they may be read by a colleague or manager within your team who may be unfamiliar with the service user and will need to be able to find and understand key information in order to respond in an emergency. Consequently it is also important that records are written in language at a basic level which is comprehensible in terms of spelling, punctuation and grammar. Although service users are not the *primary* audience for case records (Dyke, 2019) they may find some professional writing particularly difficult to understand and may need support to understand what has been written about them. Where possible case notes should avoid the use of abbreviations which service users or professionals from outside of social work might not understand. There will be times when it is important to use specialist terms, but these may need explaining, either within the note or by providing some support to help a service user understand what has been written about them. The use of specialist language is tricky as there is an inherent conflict between making case notes as accessible as possible and also ensuring that they are underpinned by professional expertise grounded in theory (Balkow and Lillis, 2019).

Including facts and professional views

As a social work student in the 1980s (writing case records by hand on paper or recording notes on a Dictaphone that were then typed up by office secretaries) I was given very clear guidance that case recording should contain only facts. Where any 'opinion' was included this was clearly marked as such to distinguish it from factual information. Opinion in this context was considered to be inherently subjective (while facts were objective) and therefore of limited value. Over the past three decades or so there has been increasing recognition that social workers should be including opinion in their recording (and assessments) and that this should be based on their professional training and expertise. It is more commonly referred to as offering a professional view rather than an opinion to clarify that this is based on objective analysis rather than a personal or uninformed opinion. A professional view should be based on the factual information presented as this provides the evidence to justify the analysis and recommendations. A case record commonly includes any or all of the following as relevant:

- facts (details of people involved, things that have been said or done and observations)
- professional view of the social worker
- the view of the service user and, where relevant, carers/family members
- a note of any dissent or disagreement from the service user
- reported information (which may include a professional view) from other professionals involved with the service user.

Looking at this list of potential components of a case record exemplifies the way in which case recording draws on a wide range of competences and is considerably more than just a record of facts. Expressing a professional view requires social workers to draw on the full range of professional capabilities (such as knowledge, critical reflection and values and ethics), gathering facts requires observation skills and presenting the view of others, including service users, requires sensitivity and linguistic skill.

Representing other people's views

As identified in the SCIE report (2016) referred to above, an awareness that a service user has the right to read what has been written about them is an important consideration for social workers when writing case records. Information should be specific and sufficiently detailed to communicate any risks or concerns even if the social worker is wary about putting information in writing as it may create or increase tensions in the working relationship with service users. To address this concern it is good practice, where possible, to ensure that any sensitive information is shared with service users before it is recorded in the files. This will not avoid the potential conflict that may arise from sharing sensitive information, but it does ensure that the service user is aware of what is being written about them and provides an opportunity for them to request that their own, potentially conflicting, perspective is recorded, as in the following case study.

Case Study (from Lillis 2017)

Case summary/Discussion (extract, 9 lines from 31 lines)

Long telephone call with Mr Y's son on his mobile.

I outlined the assessment criteria to him and discussed section 47 NHS Community Care Act 1990 in outlining the feedback from the ward sister that Mr Y is currently self-caring with regards to personal care and may not qualify for home care support.

(Continued)

(Continued)

> He suggested this judgement was scandalous and that I had been well trained in 'washing my hands', 'ticking boxes'.
>
> I advised him to put in a complaint if he was not happy with any decision made and I was wanting to support the situation.

Text 8: Case notes – email (extract 28 from 38 lines)

Morning

I wanted to make you aware of a potentially difficult situation in relation to Mr Y on Hospital Ward X

Section 2 received and Mr Y ready for discharge. I understand from the logs and discussion with HCM1 that the information is supporting the fact that Mr Y's health needs have improved since admission to the point where the OT has assessed Mr Y as independent with washing and dressing, mobilising and going to the toilet.

I contacted Mr Y's son last night suggesting that the information received is suggesting his father's needs may not satisfy 'on the appearance of need' A Section 47 assessment Care Act 1990 and consequently assessment criteria.

My understanding with regards to section 47(1)(a) requires an assessment to be carried out by the local authority whether or not the individual requests it. That is, the obligation to make an assessment for community care services does not depend on a request, but on the appearance of need.

Second, the degree of need required before the duty to assess is triggered is only 'apparent' or 'possible' need; it does not have to be 'urgent or pressing or actual need'.

Third, the duty to assess arises even if there is little prospect of the individual actually qualifying for the services, either because of resource limitations on the part of the local authority or because of the financial circumstances of the service user (R v. *Bristol City Council ex parte Penfold* [1998] 1 CCLR 315). Similarly, the duty to assess arises even when services are discretionary. My conversation with the Son was overheard by colleagues and he became angry likening my professionalism to that of the workers in the Baby P case. He was in intonation and content of speech, angry for much of the telephone conversation and efforts I made to have an open discussion to discuss discharge plans have broken down. I understand he is of the view that his fathers needs being assessed in a medical setting may not reflect how they are within a community setting and I tried to explain that I was reliant on the judgments of presenting needs.

– Thanks

There will be some occasions where there is a justification to withhold access to specific information as sharing it with a specific service user is considered to risk serious harm to them or to someone else. Restricting access in this way would only take place if there were strong grounds that access would pose a risk of serious harm.

Chapter summary

In this chapter you have considered the ways in which case recording both supports practice and is a legal and administrative duty. You have explored some of the challenges of case recording, including the shifting institutional context, the significant time pressures and the complexity of addressing service users' rights, often with interrelated family groups. Case recording, in common with all social work writing, should reflect the value base of social work. This includes maintaining public trust and being accountable but also protecting and promoting the rights of service users.

Further reading

Rai, L (2014) *Effective Writing for Social Work: Making a Difference.* Bristol: Policy Press.

This is a slightly more challenging read but contains a chapter on 'Effective Case Recording' which you may find helpful if you wanted to take your reading further.

Sidwell, N (2019) *Social Work Documentation: A Guide to Strengthening Your Case Recording.* Washington, DC: NASW Press.

This is a useful 'how to' guide with exercises and includes content on electronic case recording and client cultural differences, and it encourages individuals to reflect on personal strengths and challenges. This book is published in the USA so it will be important to be aware of national differences in legislation and practices.

8

Reports

Lucy Rai and Theresa Lillis

Introduction

Reports take many forms in social work practice and are required for a number of purposes, such as when completing an assessment or a review. Some reports are tightly
structured around digital forms while other are written based around looser templates
that allow the writer more flexibility. Using CAPS can be a very helpful way to plan your
assessment and report writing, particularly if you are in a new role, as the expectations
of these documents are highly context-specific. This chapter will introduce the reader to
interrogating the purpose of reports and the writers' role in transmitting the required
information. The intended purpose and audience will be explored, referring back to
Chapter 1, and discussion will include exploring how to balance the use of narrative,
description, evidence and professional judgement.

Reports as part of a network of documents

Chapter 7 introduced the idea that case records do not sit alone, but are associated with other documents, particularly assessment reports. Individual documents (such as a single assessment report or review) are linked in several ways:

1. A number of documents may re-use the same factual information, organised or presented in different ways.
2. Documents can be associated but created at different points in time.
3. Parts of a document may be written by different people.
4. The same document may be re-written or have associated versions for different audiences.

Case records can be viewed as the starting point for assessment and review reports as they are intended to capture events contemporaneously, as close as possible to when they happen. Assessment and review reports are created less frequently and draw together factual information and professional views, often from a range of sources. Assessment and review reports are also frequently created repeatedly over time, although the time intervals are greater than for case records. For example, where there are concerns about a child's welfare an initial review would be followed up with a more detailed 'core assessment'. Similarly there are guidelines, some of which are legal obligations, to undertake reviews of needs and services at prescribed intervals. Assessment and review reports will frequently draw on information from a number of sources. These could involve case records, emails, previous reports, the views of the service user (and their family members or carers) and views and evidence from relevant professionals, such as teachers, police officers, health professionals or residential care staff. One of the challenges of writing an assessment or review report, therefore, is to select and synthesise a wide range of information into one coherent document. One of the most important documents related to assessment reports in particular is the chronology.

Chronologies

Social work is concerned with the connectedness of social events and relationships. It is the context of a particular event which enables social workers to make sense of the situation and begin to build an assessment of associated needs, risks and opportunities or strengths. The concept of context is very broad and includes both the immediate context (social, physical, emotional). One of the most important ways in which context can be established is through the creation of a chronology. The importance of creating a clear chronology of events has been highlighted repeatedly, for example by Laming (2003), DoE (2010), Scottish Government (2012). The Care Inspectorate in Scotland has provided practice guidance on creating and using chronologies in the context of children and families, and endorses the definition offered by the National Risk Framework:

Chronologies provide a key link in the chain of understanding needs/risks, including the need for protection from harm. Setting out key events in sequential date order, they give a summary timeline of child and family circumstances [or those of an individual using adult services], patterns of behaviour and trends in lifestyle that may greatly assist any assessment and analysis. They are a logical, methodical and systematic means of organising, merging and helping make sense of information. They also help to highlight gaps and omitted details that require further exploration, investigation and assessment.

(National Risk Framework, 2012, cited in Care Inspectorate, 2017)

While the importance of chronologies has been particularly highlighted in the context of children and families, they are also of value when working with other service user groups. This definition illustrates the important role that a chronology plays in undertaking analysis needed to form an assessment, particularly when working with complex family dynamics in the context of safeguarding. Chronologies should not be an end in themselves, but rather a tool which provides vital insights when formulating assessments (Hardy, 2018; Dyke, 2019).

Using CAPS to understand an assessment report

Case study: Alex's assessment report

The following case study illustrates some of the ways in which the purpose, context, audience and contributors to reports are important. Read through the assessment report and then look at the table below and try to apply CAPS to the report.

(This is an extract from an assessment report. All of the names, places and dates have been fictionalised to preserve anonymity.)

Case Study

Extract from a single assessment report: Alex

Details of all children or young people living in household

Name	DOB	Gender	Ethnicity	Disability	Religion	Who has PR	Party record ID
Chris	Aged 8	Male	White	Not known	Not stated	Marie	
Alex (service user)	Aged 10	Male	White	Not known	Not stated	Marie	
Amy	Aged 12	Female	White	Not known	Not stated	Marie	
Phillip	Aged 14	Male	White	Not known	Not stated	Marie	

(Continued)

(Continued)

Family or other household members

Name	DOB	Gender	Ethnicity	Disability	Religion	Relation-ship to child	Party record ID
Roger	Not known	Male	White	Not known	Not stated	Father	

Social worker's views and recommendation
Section 8: (Part C) Social Worker's views

Social worker's professional judgement and risk analysis

What are we worried about (risks)

Alex was subject to a child protection plan while in the care of his father in Northshire Social Services. Northshire Social Care will be able to advise Midshire Social Services of the concerns in respect of Roger's parenting and lifestyle.

Roger does not appear to have a fixed residence at this time – Northshire social care are unclear as to his actual home address.

Alex is not registered with a GP. Alex is not accessing education. Alex has very limited clothing.

Alex has no stability and needs to have a fixed home address where he is able to settle and access health, education and social support.

Paternal and maternal grandfathers present as a risk to children and therefore no unsupervised contact should take place.

Alex's emotional well-being is of concern. Alex believed that he was living with his father, he had contact with his mother and has not heard from his father who has not collected him as arranged.

Marie will need support to be able to meet the needs of all the children in her home.

What is working well to address these worries (strengths)

Marie has a residence order and is therefore able to exercise this to allow [SU] to remain with her.

Marie is accepting of support from the children's centre for Philip.

Marie has identified and is agreeable to additional support from social care and a MAT* to be able to meet Alex's needs, including education.

Marie would like support from community outreach to ensure that all benefits would be in place. If Alex was to reside with his mother the concerns in respect of Roger's parenting would be reduced.

*MAT refers to multi-agency team

What is the impact of these risks/behaviours

Alex would have no stability if he was with his father at this time. Alex would have a fixed address and sense of belonging if he was to reside with his mother. There are concerns about the negative impact of Roger's parenting and lifestyle on Alex as this has led to Alex being subject to a child protection plan in Northshire Social Services.

Alex is not achieving his potential as he is not accessing education or interacting socially with peers.

Alex's current instability and circumstances will be impacting on his emotional well-being and sense of belonging.

Alex is not having his health needs met.

Alex needs to be protected from any adult who may present as a risk to children.

How will we know when the desired outcomes have been achieved/things are better

Alex needs stability, a permanent home where he can feel a sense of belonging.

Marie should exercise her PR and Court Order to allow Alex to reside with her on a permanent basis.

Alex needs to be registered with the GP and enrolled in an appropriate educational establishment.

Marie needs to be in receipt of all benefits for Alex.

Alex to have a bed of his own and clothes that belong to him. Alex to be free from the impact of poor parenting.

Social worker's recommendations – what needs to happen next (to address the risk, build the strengths, address the needs). Include outline Child's Plan

Northshire Social Care holds information in respect of the concerns around Roger, his parenting and lifestyle that is not fully known to Midshire Social Care at this time. The conference will be able to hear this information and it should be considered prior to a decision being made in the best interest of Alex.

At the time of writing this report it is the view of Social Care that Alex's needs would not be met to a good enough standard in the care of his father, Roger.

It is recommended therefore that it would be in the in the best interest of Alex to remain in the care of his mother, Marie. Marie has a Court Order in place in respect of residence and this would allow her to take responsibility for Alex.

Midshire Social Care feel that Alex should be supported in the care of his mother, Marie, at a Child in Need level.

Marie needs support to access education for Alex. Alex should be registered at the local health centre.

(Continued)

(Continued)

> Community Outreach to access all appropriate financial support and benefits are in place for the family. Social care will provide a bed for Alex.
>
> Social Care will provide some financial support to purchase some essential clothing for Alex.
>
> A MAT should be requested to support Alex with accessing youth groups/structured activities out of school.
>
> Marie to be supported to further develop her parenting skills to be able to support the older children. The support in place for the younger children from the children's centre should continue.

Activity 8.1

Find an assessment that you have been involved with, or ask someone in your agency if you can look at a completed assessment. Try and complete the same CAPS table for your own assessment, referring to the example above based on Alex.

Table 8.1 CAPS assessment

		Ask yourself . . .	Answer based on Alex's assessment
C	Context	Are there any specific requirements arising from the agency or service user group that I am writing my report for? Is there specific software or a template that my agency requires me to use for this report? Are there policies around timescales for completing or signing off the report?	
A	Audience	Who is the report primarily written for? Who else may read all or extracts from the report, either now or in the future?	
P	Purpose	What is the purpose of the report? Why is it required (is there a legal duty associated with it)? What is the outcome that I want the report to achieve?	
S	Self	What is my role as I write this report? Which aspects of my identity are relevant?	

Identifying the purpose

Before you begin to write a report it is important to pause and reflect on why you are writing it. It is not enough to begin only with the knowledge that the report is required, often by law as this will not help you focus on *how* to write. When thinking about the purpose it is worth asking yourself the following questions:

- Who is the report primarily about?
- What are the events which resulted in the need for this report? Are you clear about preceding events, whether they took place over a few days or even hours, or if this engagement follows several months or even years without significant intervention?
- What are the possible consequences of the report? These might include the provision of withdrawal of services or financial support, legal action or maintenance of the current situation.
- What is your role in the assessment or review? Are you providing expert advice? Are you acting on behalf of a statutory agency which has responsibility for providing resources? Do you have case management responsibility?
- What outcomes do you, using your professional knowledge, want to come from the report?

If you are not clear about the purpose, or any of these questions it is worth discussing this with your line manager or supervisor prior to beginning to plan your writing. The more clarity you have about the purpose of a report the clearer it is likely to be for your readers.

Audience

The audience for a report normally involves a range of people including the service user, carers/family and a potentially large number of other professionals who are involved in providing a service, either at the time, in the past or in the future. As with case recording, reports remain documents which may be referred back to in the future and so the audience is not predictable.

Activity 8.2

Consider the following three case studies and the people involved in each who are potential readers of social work reports. For each one note down any considerations you would need to keep in mind to make sure that your report was accessible and relevant for them. For each would there be anything you might not want them to read?

Case Study

Rebecca

Rebecca has been referred to social services by her school as a result of behavioural changes. The report is based on an initial assessment, which concluded that Rebecca

(Continued)

(Continued)

was a child in need but not at risk. She lives with her mother (who has parental responsibility) and her mother's partner. Rebecca has no contact with her father, but she has an elder half-brother (aged 12) who lives with his father and stepmother. There is a blank table here for you to try and complete but below you will find a table with some examples completed for you.

Reader	What to keep in mind?	Anything you wouldn't want them to read?
Rebecca		
Rebecca's mother		
Rebecca's mother's partner		
Paul		
Paul's parents		
Rebecca's head teacher		
Your line manager		
Rebecca's school nurse		
Police officer from the child protection team		

Comment

Reader	What to keep in mind? Anything you wouldn't want them to read?
Rebecca	At 5 years old Rebecca's reading will be limited as will her understanding. It is, however, important that she understands some of what is being discussed about her welfare and that she is able to contribute her own wishes and feelings in an age appropriate way, such as through play or drawing. She may need time to both express her wishes and feelings as well as for you to explain the report to her. As this is an initial assessment there will be limited time for building a trusting relationship with Rebecca and as the focus will be on immediate risk, some of this work may take place in the fuller assessment that will follow.
Rebecca's mother	Rebecca's mother has parental responsibility; Rebecca is also in her full-time care. As a result she should be fully involved and informed. She has no communication or comprehension needs, but the focus of the report might be distressing and confusing. She may not be familiar with some terms or references to people or services mentioned, so it will be good practice to allow time for her to read a draft of the report with you so that you can explain anything she doesn't understand. If Rebecca's mother disagrees with any facts or recommendations, these should be noted in the report.
Rebecca's mother's partner	This person does not have parental responsibility and as such does not have a right to read the report. However, he is resident with Rebecca and her mother so it may be relevant to include information provided by him.

Reader	What to keep in mind? Anything you wouldn't want them to read?
Philip	Paul is of an age and level of understanding to be able to read his case records. However, this assessment relates only to Rebecca. There will be a cross reference in Paul's case recording as he visits his mother's home, but Paul would not have a right to read the report about Rebecca.
Rebecca's head teacher	
Your line manager	
Rebecca's school nurse	
Police officer from the child protection team	

Case Study

Conran

Conran is 15 and has been a looked-after child for 18 months. He is currently living in a foster placement but has experienced several moves. He has irregular contact with his mother only, who shares parental responsibility with the local authority and has intermittent mental health problems and a low level of literacy. Conran has had erratic school attendance and has been involved in some petty crime. This report is for a regular Looked-After Child review.

Reader	What to keep in mind?	Anything you wouldn't want them to read?
Conran		
Conran's mother		
Conran's foster carers		
Your line manager		
Conran's teacher		
Youth offending officer		
Education welfare officer		
Conran's GP		

Case Study

Amrit

Amrit is 78 and was diagnosed with dementia three months ago. His first language is Punjabi but he speaks English reasonably well. He is currently living at home with the support of his daughter, Mala. This report is for an assessment to consider Amrit's care needs as Mala is moving house for work and will no longer be able to provide the support that Amrit needs. Mala speaks fluent English and works as a lawyer.

Reader	What to keep in mind?	Anything you wouldn't want them to read?
Amrit		
Mala		
Amrit's GP		
Nurse from older adults community mental health team		
Your line manager		

Selection and synthesis

As already discussed reports generally draw on information from a wide range of sources, some of which you may have written and some of which have been written by others. The idea of selecting and synthesising information from a range of sources was introduced in Chapter 3 in the context of writing an academic essay. The process of selecting and synthesising sources for a report is similar, although the sources and purpose of the document are different. Figure 8.1 illustrates the kinds of sources commonly drawn on when preparing an academic assignment.

Figure 8.2 illustrates some of the typical sources of information drawn on when preparing an assessment or report. You will see that, unlike academic assignments, not all of these sources are written. Important information will also be gathered from observations and discussions with the service user and any family or carers. The information from these sources would normally also be written down, such as in a case record. Similarly, evidence from other professionals may initially be shared verbally, perhaps in a meeting, but would then also be captured in writing, for example in the minutes of a meeting or an entry in a case record.

Whether writing an academic assignment or a report in practice, therefore, you will often have a significant amount of *potential* evidence or information to draw on. In both contexts you will need to review possible sources of evidence, select what to include or draw on, and then synthesise this information into one coherent document. This process requires the author to use their professional knowledge, experience and analysis in order to select the most relevant evidence to put forward in their professional view or assessment of a situation. When writing a report it is important to recognise that your role is not only to present objective information in a coherent way, but to make a case or an argument based on your professional judgement.

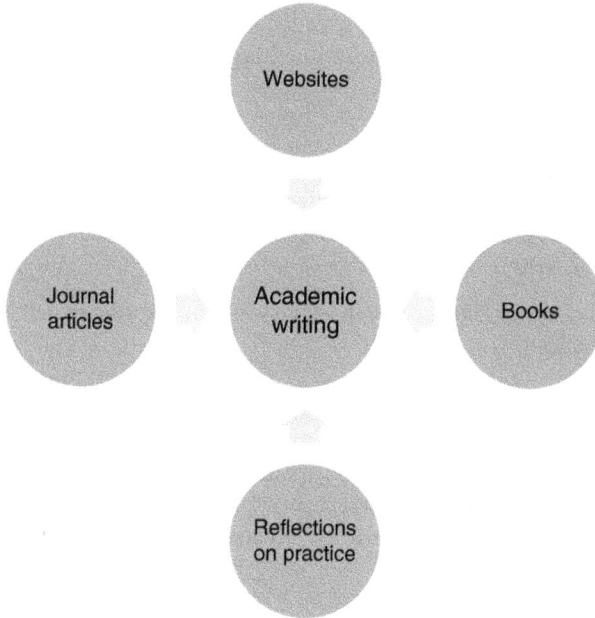

Figure 8.1 Typical sources for an academic assignment

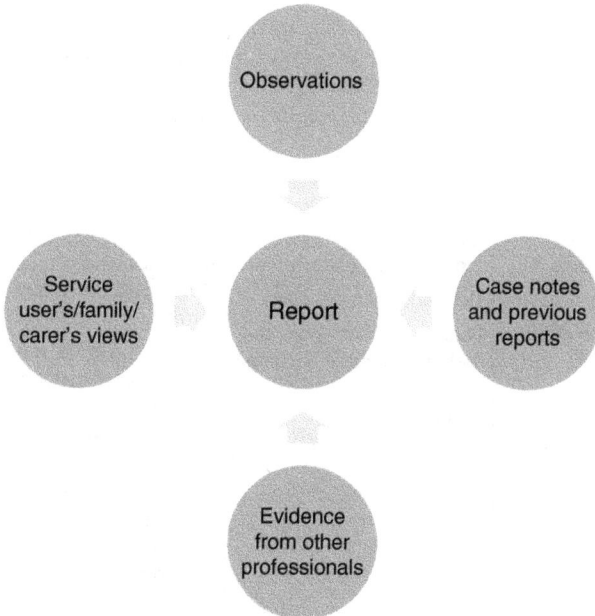

Figure 8.2 Sources for a report

Persuasive writing

Academic assignments and reports are both examples of persuasive, or what is sometimes referred to as rhetorical, writing. Persuasive writing aims to persuade the audience or reader of a particular perspective or course of action based on evidence and argument. Katz (2018) suggests that the origins of rhetorical writing lie in the Classical Greek concepts of pathos, logos and ethos:

Pathos   Refers to the use of emotion to engage and persuade the reader.

Logos   Involves persuading the reader through logic and reasoning based on evidence and argument. Logos is also closely associated with the credibility of the writer.

Ethos   Refers to adapting the way in which you write in order to persuade a particular audience.

Ethos resonates with the concept of audience in CAPS, and there is also a relationship between logos and self, your credibility as an author. You will find further discussion of both argumentation (logos) and emotion (pathos) throughout this book, but here the focus is on the ways in which an awareness of pathos, logos and ethos can be helpful when writing a text intended to persuade the reader of a particular point view.

Activity 8.3

For this activity look again at Alex's single assessment report which you read earlier in this chapter and is duplicated here. You may also like to repeat this exercise with a report that you have written yourself. Read the report through again and as you read try to identify any of the following features:

Pathos	Logos	Ethos
Use of emotive words or phrases in the context of: Describing events or observations Emphasising urgency or seriousness Stressing a recommendation Using direct words of others, such as service users, which contain emotive language	Identification of the writer's status Language which indicates the expertise of the writer Reference to evidence Language which indicates that an argument is being constructed Professional recommendation/view expressed	Does the language used suggest who the intended reader(s) are? Are complex or specialist words used including jargon or acronyms? Who would understand these terms? Has language been used which would take account of a particular service user, such as a child, someone with a disability or who speaks English as a second or additional language? Based on the language used, who do you think is the *primary* audience the writer is trying to convince or persuade?

Details of all children or young people living in household

Name	DOB	Gender	Ethnicity	Disability	Religion	Who has PR	Party Record ID
Chris	Aged 8	Male	White	Not known	Not stated	Marie	
Alex (service user)	Aged 10	Male	White	Not known	Not stated	Marie	
Amy	Aged 12	Female	White	Not known	Not stated	Marie	
Phillip	Aged 14	Male	White	Not known	Not stated	Marie	

Family or other household members

Name	DOB	Gender	Ethnicity	Disability	Religion	Relation-ship to child	Party record ID
Roger	Not known	Male	White	Not known	Not stated	Father	

Social Worker's Views and Recommendation

Section 8: (Part C) Social Worker's views

Social worker's professional judgement and risk analysis

What are we worried about (risks)?

Alex was subject to a child protection plan while in the care of his father in Northshire Social Services. Northshire Social Care will be able to advise Midshire Social Services of the concerns in respect of Roger's parenting and lifestyle.

Roger does not appear to have a fixed residence at this time – Northshire Social Care are unclear as to his actual home address.

Alex is not registered with a GP. Alex is not accessing education. Alex has very limited clothing.

Alex has no stability and needs to have a fixed home address where he is able to settle and access health, education and social support.

Paternal and maternal grandfathers present as a risk to children and therefore no unsupervised contact should take place.

Alex's emotional well-being is of concern. Alex believed that he was living with his father, he had contact with his mother and has not heard from his father who has not collected him as arranged.

Marie will need support to be able to meet the needs of all the children in her home.

(Continued)

(Continued)

What is working well to address these worries (strengths)?

> Marie has a residence order and is therefore able to exercise this to allow Alex to remain with her.
>
> Marie is accepting of support from the children's centre for Philip.
>
> Marie has identified and is agreeable to additional support from social care and a MAT to be able to meet Alex's needs, including education.
>
> Marie would like support from community outreach to ensure that all benefits will be in place.
>
> If Alex were to reside with his mother the concerns in respect of Roger's parenting would be reduced.

What is the impact of these risks/behaviours?

> Alex would have no stability if he was with his father at this time. Alex would have a fixed address and sense of belonging if he was to reside with his mother. There are concerns about the negative impact of Roger's parenting and lifestyle on Alex as this has led to Alex being subject to a child protection plan in Northshire Social Services.
>
> Alex is not achieving his potential as he is not accessing education or interacting socially with peers.
>
> Alex's current instability and circumstances will be impacting on his emotional well-being and sense of belonging.
>
> Alex is not having his health needs met.
>
> Alex needs to be protected from any adult who may present as a risk to children.

How will we know when the desired outcomes have been achieved/things are better?

> Alex needs stability, a permanent home where he can feel a sense of belonging.
>
> Marie should exercise her PR and Court Order to allow Alex to reside with her on a permanent basis.
>
> Alex needs to be registered with the GP and enrolled in an appropriate educational establishment.
>
> Marie needs to be in receipt of all benefits for Alex.
>
> Alex to have a bed of his own and clothes that belong to him. Alex to be free from the impact of poor parenting.

Social worker's recommendations – what needs to happen next (to address the risk, build the strengths, address the needs). Include outline child's plan

Northshire Social Care holds information in respect of the concerns around Roger, his parenting and lifestyle that is not fully known to Midshire Social Care at this time. The conference will be able to hear this information and it should be considered prior to a decision being made in the best interest of Alex.

At the time of writing this report it is the view of Social Care that Alex's needs would not be met to a good enough standard in the care of his father, Roger.

It is recommended therefore that it would be in the in the best interest of Alex to remain in the care of his mother, Marie. Marie has a Court Order in place in respect of residence and this would allow her to take responsibility for Alex.

Midshire Social Care feel that Alex should be supported in the care of his mother, Marie, at a Child in Need level.

Marie needs support to access education for Alex. Alex should be registered at the local health centre.

Community Outreach to access all appropriate financial support and benefits are in place for the family. Social care will provide a bed for Alex.

Social care will provide some financial support to purchase some essential clothing for Alex.

A MAT should be requested to support Alex with accessing youth groups/structured activities out of school.

Marie to be supported to further develop her parenting skills to be able to support the older children. The support in place for the younger children from the children's centre should continue.

Comment

This report extract does not include any direct emotive words and most of the language is explicitly not emotive. The full report does include words such as 'aggressive', but it is important to consider whether the use of specific words are neutrally descriptive or imply a judgement intended to have an emotive impact. Logos is mostly evident in the processes that surround the assessment form itself. For example, only a social worker can complete the form which grants them an authority as the writer. Recommendations are included in the assessment (see the final box entitled 'Social worker's recommendations') and these are written in the third person, which has the impact of distancing the writer from the recommendations. To illustrate, the report states that 'It is the view of Social Care that Alex's needs would not be met to a good enough standard in the care of his father, Roger.' By using the phrase 'it is the view of Social Care' rather than 'It is my view' or even 'It is my professional view', the social worker clearly indicates the institutional status of the report and that they are writing on behalf of their agency. The ethos of the writing indicates an intention to be accessible to the intended reader through the use

(Continued)

(Continued)

of simple everyday language. There is some use of technical/specialist terms and a couple of abbreviations are used but in the main the report is written in simple, accessible language. Some words used do have a particular meaning in the context of social work, for example 'stability', 'sense of belonging', which would be understood by health and social care colleagues but perhaps less so by service users. There are also some terms which have a legal significance, such as 'child protection plan', 'fixed residence' and 'residence order', which may not be clear to all service users. The only abbreviation which may not be commonly understood is 'MAT' which refers to a 'multi-agency team'.

You may not have thought about reports as being persuasive, and may feel uncomfortable about the idea of your role as a social worker being to persuade others of a particular course of action. Thinking of a report as being persuasive does not imply that the author is being subjective, biased or manipulative. It does recognise that your role as a social worker is to:

- be clear and confident about your professional expertise
- collate and synthesise information, including gathering the views of the service user, family/carers and other professionals
- undertake an analysis drawing on your professional experience and knowledge (including theory, legislation and policy)
- arrive at a professional view which balances all parties' rights, responsibilities and risks.

It is this professional view that should guide the persuasive stance of the report and result in a recommendation. There may be times when a report might offer more than one possible course of action, or indeed no action at all, but in all cases the conclusion reached should be based on a well-argued and evidenced professional view.

Writing a persuasive document does raise ethical issues, primarily the power that the social worker has when compiling an assessment or review and capturing this in a report. As with all social work practice it is important that this power is recognised and managed ethically, rather than denying its existence. McDonald et al. suggest that *If used ethically, persuasive writing is not about trickery or manipulation but about targeting information for a client-centred result* (2015, p371). To achieve ethical persuasive writing the imbalances of power need to be recognised in order to allow all relevant voices to be represented. A persuasive report should not exclude the views of, for example, the service user or carer. There will be occasions where you are aware that the service user or a carer might disagree with your evaluation and recommendations. Such differences in view should be included openly, but it is the role of the social worker to weigh up all of the views and evidence in order to make a recommendation. This difficult work is an integral part of social work practice; the writing only reflects the practice through an articulation of the analysis and professional view offered.

Professional voice

Voice is often used to refer to the ways in which we refer to ourselves in writing and our actions (for example *I visited* Maria Perez or Maria Perez *was visited*) and how we refer to others (for example as *Maria Perez, Mrs Perez* or *Mum*). In writing social work texts, you make lots of small choices (about the use of a particular word) or big choices (about how to build an evidence-based argument) when representing yourself and others. The phrase *professional voice* underlines the fact that what you write and how you write it carry a particular weight – the perspectives and accounts written by social workers have profound consequences for people's lives, such as whether a child should be separated from the adults(s) she is living with or whether an elderly person will receive basic care. The language that is used is therefore of crucial importance. In this section you are asked to reflect on different aspects of voice.

Your voice

Activity 8.4 (from https:/wisper.writinginsocialwork.com/resource/voice-in-writing/)

Look at the examples below. Use the table to identify the particular way the social worker chooses to express her/his voice and to consider why.

- *I would strongly recommend that the children are placed on child protection plans.*
- *It was agreed there should be an adjournment.*
- *Jane disclosed that her mother sexually abused her between the ages of 6 and 10.*
- *Her son gave her 'a dirty look'.*

VOICE	Examples	Why write in this way?
1. Written in first person singular		
2. Written in third person		
3. Written in impersonal third person/passive		
4. Use of quotations		

Comment

VOICE	Examples	Why write in this way?
1. Written in first person singular	*I would strongly recommend that the children are placed on child protection plans.*	*To emphasise the social worker's professional evaluation.*

(Continued)

(Continued)

VOICE	Examples	Why write in this way?
2. **Written in third person**	*Jane disclosed that her mother sexually abused her between the ages of 6 and 10.*	*To report an account by someone else.*
3. **Written in impersonal third person/passive**	*It was agreed there should be an adjournment.*	*To indicate that a decision was made/ possibly to indicate that others were involved in the decision/evaluation.*
4. **Use of quotations**	*Her son gave her 'a dirty look'.*	*To indicate that a social worker is using everyday language to present an account.*

There is often concern expressed about the lack of an explicit professional voice in social work writing, for example a greater use of the impersonal third person/passive as in Example 3 than the use of the first person in Example 1. The language used in Example 3 might be used for a number of reasons, including wanting to indicate that the decision was not made by the social worker alone. But one effect of using the third person impersonal/passive is that the reader may not be clear about the social worker's view on a situation. Other uses of language can also background a social worker's perspective: for example 'hedging language' such as 'really' in the statement *The lunch time and tea time calls are not really required* (Lillis 2017). The 'not really' is also ambiguous because it is unclear whether the calls are needed or not.

Giving a clear and unambiguous evaluation of a situation (however complex) is a challenging but crucial professional purpose of social worker writing. The social worker's professional perspective needs to come through in the language used. One reason given for social workers' backgrounding their position in writing is the larger social context in which social work takes place and the way in which social workers are often unfairly criticised (for example in the media) leading to some fearing to state their view, or what has been described as 'defensive recording' (Garcia-Maza et al., 2010; Balkow and Lillis, 2019). Professional social workers play a crucial role in supporting people and the language they use in their writing to present theirs and others' views will have an effect on decisions and future actions.

The voices of others

Of course, in presenting their professional perspective social workers represent the views of others.

One key way in which social workers present the voices of service users is to include direct quotations from what people have said. Read the examples below. In each case, the social worker quotes a word or words used by the service user (shown in each example within speech marks '...'). Why do you think the social worker chose to quote the service user's actual words?

1. Jim has told Freya to tell social care that the children are 'full of shit' and have lied about him.
2. Beth describes that her mother was 'completely devoted' to the children.
3. Laura came down stairs mum shouted at her to get back in her room – Laura screamed 'no!' Mum went up to her and said are 'you gonna stop this behaviour?'
4. When I asked Louis, 'where do you live?', Louis's initial response was 'a street', I asked Louis where the street was and he said 'near a beach'. I asked Louis again later in the conversation 'where do you live?' and he stated 'Valley Road'.

We cannot know just from the text extracts alone why a social worker may have used direct quotations to represent the service user's perspectives and accounts. Here we offer some possible reasons. As you read, consider the extent to which you agree with the reasons given or what other reasons there may be.

- to provide a more precise sense of the context of a conversation (e.g. to show the exchange in Example 3 is heated)
- to emphasise the person's perspective and possibly distinguish it from the social worker's perspective (e.g. Example 2 shows what Beth thought)
- to provide a more precise sense of the contextual of a conversation and indicate a particular behaviour (e.g. Example 1 indicates aggression on the part of Jim)
- to provide evidence for the social worker's analysis – this could apply to any of the examples. (In Example 4, the social worker reports the conversation almost word for word to illustrate how Louis is struggling to remember details such as where he lives.)

(Extracts and discussion from https://wisper.writinginsocialwork.com/
resource/quoting-service-users/)

Social workers need to act ethically in their representation of others' views, accounts and perspectives and using direct quotations from what others have said is just one way in which social workers represent other voices in their writing. The WiSP project has developed a website which contains learning material to support students and practitioners in developing their professional writing. The WiSPER site contains more examples of how views are represented in writing (http://wisper.writinginsocialwork.com/).

Writing in the voice of the service user

A key goal in social work is to ensure that individuals, their concerns, needs and well-being are at the heart of any decisions and actions. This goal is captured in phrases such as 'Putting People First' (Department of Health, 2007, *Putting People First: A Shared Vision and Commitment to the Transformation of Adult Social Care*). One related policy and practice in adult care – often referred to as 'personalisation' – involves individuals taking active control over their needs, including organising their own care and budgets for their care.

Some written texts reflect this emphasis on the individual in the templated headings which are in the first person of the service user and require a first-person response:

My ability to participate in the assessment and support planning process . . .

I have substantial difficulty with . . .

Activity 8.5

Read the extracts below from an assessment report in the first person of the service user. Make a note of all references to the service user in the first person (I, me, my . . .).
As you read reflect on the following questions:

1. What effect does a first person report have on the reader?
2. To what extent do you think it helps to keep the person more central?
3. Would it have a different effect if written in the third person (she, her . . .)?

At times I cannot go out far on my own due to my anxiety.

I need additional support with personal care, domestic duties and support to manage my mental health.

I would like my PA (personal assistant) with me to support me when I go out especially when I shop, collect my money so that I feel like I can cope and be prepared if anything happens.

I have history of being suicidal and it is important that I have additional support to talk things through with someone close to me, who understands me, knows me well.

Writing reports in the voice of the person using a service – using **I** and talking about **my** needs – was a significant change in practice. One key benefit of the social worker writing in the voice of the service user is that it can humanise a report, reminding the reader that the written texts are about a real person with individual needs and wishes. Of course completing a form in the voice of a service user also presents key challenges. A key question to consider is the extent to which it is ethical to write in the voice of the service user, particularly if a service user is unable to verbally express themselves or doesn't want to do so.

Chapter summary

In this chapter you have considered the ways in which reports sit within a network of linked documents, including case notes and chronologies. You will encounter reports in various contexts, including in the process of completing assessments, reviews and court hearings, and CAPS provides a starting place for considering how to approach a specific report. What all reports share is that they should conclude with a recommendation based on your professional judgement. The case studies shared here illustrate the importance of gathering and synthesising evidence in order to present a professional view and recommendation. Presenting this evidence involves writing persuasively, and in this chapter you have been introduced to some of the techniques which can be useful in rhetorical writing. One key element of evidence is the voice of the service user and their family, whose views may differ from each other and from your own. Presenting the views of service users – and sometimes those of other professionals – alongside your own can be one of the most challenging aspects of effective report writing.

Further reading

Watt, J (2013) *Report Writing for Social Workers*. London: Sage.

A useful overview of report writing in social work which leads the reader through the process of writing a report and includes plenty of activities.

WiSPeR (2020) available at http://wisper.writinginsocialwork.com/ (accessed 11 August 2020).

This is a free online resource which contains activities and videos developed by the WiSP team in collaboration with social workers and educators in social work.

9
Writing for court

Introduction

The writing undertaken in the context of legal proceedings is important. It requires social workers to use their professional judgement to advise courts and tribunals considering important decisions about the welfare of vulnerable people. There are commonly multiple audiences and contributors when writing for court and the social workers can therefore be the orchestrator of complex texts which nonetheless need to communicate to the court clearly and convincingly. This chapter will outline some of the relevant statutory guidance and identify the challenges of writing for courts and tribunals and explain how an understanding of audience, persuasive writing and the use of evidence can result in more effective writing.

Who writes for the court and why?

Any social worker, whether working in the statutory, private or third sector, could be called upon to write a statement for court. Statutory social workers, however, have specific duties in relation to court work and are more likely to write for court as a routine element of their work. Court work can be complex and although you will study relevant legislation and guidance during your qualifying programme, in most cases statutory social workers will be supported and advised by your local authority solicitor. It is natural for involvement in court work to generate anxiety for many people. However, as a student or newly qualified social worker you would normally be protected from taking on responsibility for court work and regardless of our level of experience key decisions will be made alongside a senior member of the team, such as a team manager. All documents, whether written specifically for court or collated from existing documents and submitted to court, should also be signed off by a senior member of your team. The aim of this chapter, therefore, is to introduce you to the important role that writing plays in court work and to explain some of the ways in which you can make this writing as effective as possible.

Activity 9.1

There are many situations in which a social worker might need to write a document for court. Have a look at the following list of actions and the list of teams that you might work in as a social worker. The names of the teams may vary where you practise, but taking the area of responsibility generally, try to match them up and identify the primary legislation which governs the action:

- care proceedings
- mental health tribunal
- application to the court of protection
- pre-sentence reports.

Team	Action	Legislation
Youth offending team		
Children's team		
Adults' team		
Mental health team		

There are of course many other teams and kinds of actions but these are some of the main ways in which social workers interact with the courts, for example evidence in decisions about adoption. Children's teams are responsible for child protection or safeguarding, which frequently involves taking care proceedings. This is a very wide area governed in England and Wales by the Children Act 1989 and the Children and Families Act 2014. There is an example of an extract from a care proceedings court report on a child we are calling 'Chanice' in Activity 9.2 below. You may find it helpful to have a brief look at this now, but you will return to it later in this chapter when care proceedings will be addressed in some detail. Statements produced as part of care proceedings are one of the most common ways in which social workers write and prepare documentation for the court. The statements and associated documentation that social workers write for family courts are governed by the Family Procedure Rules 2010. Part 22 of these Rules give detailed guidance on preparing evidence for court, including written statements. They include how to structure a statement, the details that should be included and supporting documents (referred to as exhibits) that should be submitted (Family Procedure Rules 2010).

Social workers may be called upon to write an application to the Court of Protection if an adult is considered to be in need of protection and is not able to make their own decisions due to their mental capacity (Mental Capacity Act 2005). This could apply whether you are working with an older person, someone with a disability or mental health needs. People with mental health problems who are considered to be at risk to themselves or others and do not agree to assessment or treatment voluntarily may be subject to one of the sections of the Mental Health Act 1983. This could result in them being compulsorily detained for assessment (section 2) or treatment (section 3). One of the contexts in which social workers may be called upon to write a social circumstances report for the Court of Protection is when someone who has been detained under the Mental Health Act submits an appeal (Judiciary UK, 2013). Pre-sentence reports are written by the youth offenders team but there are also circumstances when the court may request these for adults, for example where there is an identified mental disorder, which would include people with mental health problems as well as learning disabilities (Sentencing Council, 2019). Pre-sentence reports for adults are completed by the probation service but where social workers in mental health or adult teams are working with an offender the probation officer would liaise with them in the completion of the report.

Courts require written evidence from social workers in order to understand the context and circumstances of a case being considered. For example, pre-sentence reports are required in criminal proceedings which are usually heard in the magistrates or youth court for 10–17 year olds. Only the most serious adult cases would be heard in the crown court – it is very rare for cases involving a child to be considered by the crown court, although for very serious offences they may be referred up from the youth court for sentencing. All matters relating to children are considered by the court and where the action is taken by the local authority these would be dealt with in the family court and are treated as 'public law'. Family matters which the local authority is not involved with, such as contact arrangements following a divorce, are also dealt with in the Family Court but treated as 'private law' as the dispute is between private individuals rather than a private individual and a public body, in this case the local authority (Courts and Tribunals Judiciary, 2020). In both contexts the role of the social worker is as an expert who is providing advice and guidance based on their experience and professional expertise based on research. To begin to think about your role in writing for court the next section applies CAPS to writing for criminal and care proceedings.

Using CAPS to plan your writing for court

In this section CAPS is applied to three examples of situations in which social workers are required to write a report for court. These are not the only contexts when courts may require a report from the local authority but they are perhaps the most common. Reports are not the only documents that a court might require you to submit but they are the main document that is written specifically for court. Other documents, depending on the context, can include:

- assessment reports
- review reports
- chronologies
- extracts of case recordings.

These associated documents are not considered in detail in this chapter as they are discussed elsewhere in the book, but it is important to be aware that reports do not stand alone but are supported by other documents.

Activity 9.2

You should now be familiar with CAPS and so will recognise that it is applied very generically here. If you were required to write a report in your own practice you would need to apply the model in more detail to the specific individual you were working with.

Read through the following three case study examples and identify what is common across all three situations where a report is required. For the first example, care proceedings for a child, refer to the extracts from the report provided on 'Chanice', copy the table below and try to complete it with the specific details relevant to this report.

Case Study

Illustration of a court report

Note: These are extracts from an authentic report drawn from the WiSP project (http://writinginsocialwork.com/). All names, dates and potentially identifying information have been changed to protect the anonymity of all involved.

A. Statement of the order(s) sought

The local authority is seeking a Special Guardianship Order in favour of Iris, paternal grandmother to Chanice. Chanice is already residing with Iris on an Interim Child Arrangement Order that was granted by the court on 19 May 2016.

Chanice's mother, Carol, presented very late to health services regarding her pregnancy and continued to have sporadic and inconsistent engagement with all services involved. Carol continued to use illicit substances throughout the pregnancy, namely heroin and crack cocaine, 3–5 bags per day, along with methadone and queried alcohol use. She was of no fixed abode and made no preparations for the arrival of Chanice.

[This section is not included in this extract to preserve anonymity.]

B. The range of powers available to the court under the Act in the proceedings in question (Special Guardianship Order).

[This section is not included in this extract to preserve anonymity.]

C. Precipitating events were outlined in the Initial Statement of Mrs Joan Fletcher dated 19 March 2016.

[This section is not included in this extract to preserve anonymity.]

D. The local authority has considered the Parenting Assessment of Carol dated 27 April 2016 with a negative outcome. This Parenting Assessment report is available to read in conjunction with this statement.

1. Chanice is a 6-month-old girl who is completely dependent on her carers to tend to all of her basic care needs. Chanice requires a stable, nurturing and safe environment where she will have opportunity to grow, develop and thrive. Chanice requires a carer who will prioritise her needs and welfare above their own and be responsive to her methods of communication and health requirements and in tune with her natural routine.

2. Chanice is of mixed heritage. Her birth family speak English and do not currently practise any religion. During the pregnancy with Chanice, her mother neglected her needs in that she was not monitored by health professionals to ensure her growth and development were in line with expected rates. Chanice was exposed to illicit substance use on a daily basis in the form of heroin and crack cocaine. Chanice was also exposed to methadone.

3. Chanice spent approximately 12 weeks in foster care when she was born before moving to reside with his paternal grandmother, Iris. Her needs have been consistently met in both placements.

4. Chanice does not have any outstanding or ongoing health or developmental needs for which medical intervention is required, though she is still very young to be assessed for any ongoing issues.

5. Chanice is not of an age where education is a factor in her care, though Iris will be encouraged to attend baby groups/clinics with Chanice to encourage socialisation, interaction and stimulation in a different environment.

6. Chanice is not of an age where she is able to express her likes and dislikes. She should therefore be provided opportunity to experience different activities and explore appropriately to enable her to develop her sense of self.

7. Carol has a history of self-harming behaviours linked to anxiety and depression. She was not taking medication for this.

8. Contact has taken place between Carol and Chanice on a fortnightly basis. This takes place in the prison that Carol is in, currently Ridgeleys. The contact logs report that Carol demonstrates good emotional warmth towards Chanice and is responsive to her needs. There have been no concerns raised but it is an unusually artificial environment due to the limitations in place as a result of the venue.

9. Carol has engaged with professionals since the PLO meeting (Public Law Outline); prior to this her engagement was very poor. There are concerns that when Carol is released from prison her engagement will again reduce. Carol has struggled to prioritise anything over her substance use, meaning she leads a very chaotic and unstable lifestyle.

10. Brent (father) has engaged with services on a superficial level; he has been clear from the outset that he does not wish to be assessed as sole carer for Chanice and wants Chanice to be cared for by Iris.

(Continued)

(Continued)

E.   Analysis of why there is a gap between parental capacity and the child's needs.

The local authority has considered the following when analysing the gap between parental capacity and Chanice's needs:

1.   Carol was not engaging with health services to monitor the growth or development of Chanice during pregnancy, despite raised concerns around the growth of Chanice.
2.   Carol did not make any preparations for the arrival of Chanice.
3.   The pregnancy was unplanned and Carol did not have a place to live or a steady income (she was not claiming appropriate benefits but living on hand-outs and food parcels) and had a significant addiction to substances where she was using 3–5 wraps of heroin and crack cocaine per day alongside methadone.
4.   Carol has been unable to demonstrate an ability to prioritise a child's needs over her own.
5.   The lack of commitment to finding a home for herself and Chanice or preparing for her arrival even when services were involved and offering support in this area.
6.   The lack of engagement with the MAT (Multi-Agency Team) and social care when trying to complete the pre-birth assessment.
7.   The position of both Carol and Brent in that they are not in a position to provide care to Chanice.

F.   Assessment of other significant adults who may be carers.

[This section is not included in this extract to preserve anonymity.]

G.   The ascertainable wishes and feelings of the child concerned.

[This section is not included in this extract to preserve anonymity.]

H.   Child's physical, emotional and educational needs.

[This section is not included in this extract to preserve anonymity.]

I.   The likely effect on the child of any change in circumstances.

[This section is not included in this extract to preserve anonymity.]

J.   Age, sex, background and any characteristics which the court considers relevant.

[This section is not included in this extract to preserve anonymity.]

K.   Any harm which the child has suffered or is at risk of suffering.

[This section is not included in this extract to preserve anonymity]

L.   Evidence and assessment necessary and outstanding.

[This section is not included in this extract to preserve anonymity.]

Care proceedings for a child

C	Context	At a simple level the context is a report written for court in order to support a particular action. The background to taking such an action will often be complex and be the culmination of protracted work with a family, or indeed follow an intensive but fast emergency action. The nature of your report will depend on the specific action that is being taken as the expectations of the judge will be different for emergency action compared with action that arises out of attempted partnership working with a family over a period of time.
A	Audience	The primary audience is the judge, although your report will also be read by the family and legal representatives for the local authority and the parent(s) and child.
P	Purpose	Your report is in effect an expert witness statement and its purpose is to provide the judge with information to assist in making a judgement on the case. Your report should be informed by your professional expertise in selecting and presenting evidence drawn from the facts about the circumstances and research to back up your recommendations.
S	Self	Your report should reflect your professional view and judgement and you should be prepared to be questioned on the evidence you present and the basis for the judgements that you make. You may receive advice and guidance from the local authority solicitor and the report may need to be signed off by your line manager, but it must still represent your own professional judgement. (Baynes, 2017)

Chanice's report

C	Context	
A	Audience	
P	Purpose	
S	Self	

The following examples relate to pre-sentence reports, reports for the Court of Protection and Mental Health Tribunal reports.

Pre-sentence report for a young person

C	Context	In simple terms the context is as part of the sentencing process for a young person who has been convicted of an offence. The specific context of each young person will be different. For example, you may have been working with the person for a long period of time and there may be a history of offending and/or vulnerability which needs to be considered in sentencing.
A	Audience	The primary audience is the judge, although your report will also be read by the young person, their legal representative and the legal representative for the prosecution, and the court officials. It may also be seen by the young person's parents and social worker.
P	Purpose	Your report is in effect an expert witness statement and its purpose is to provide the judge with information to assist in making a judgement on the context of the offence, including an assessment of the level of risk to the community and of serious harm to others, and also risks to the child's safety or well-being (Youth Justice Board, 2020). Your report should be informed by your professional expertise in selecting and presenting evidence drawn from facts about the circumstances and research to back up your recommendations.
S	Self	Your report should reflect your professional view and judgement and you should be prepared to be questioned on the evidence you present and the basis for the judgements that you make. You may receive advice and guidance from the local authority solicitor and the report may need to be signed off by your line manager, but it must still represent your own professional judgement. (Baynes, 2017)

Report for Court of Protection

C	Context	The Court of Protection can require a report from the local authority under section 49 of the Mental Capacity Act 2005, either because the authority has expert evidence or is bringing the case to court. The general purpose of this legislation is to enable decisions to be made on behalf of an adult who is deemed, either temporarily or permanently, not to have the mental capacity to make decisions for themselves. The specific context will depend on the individual concerned and the nature (length and extent) of involvement with the social work team.
A	Audience	The primary audience is the judge, although your report will also be read by the subject of the action and their legal representative and may be shared with anyone who the judge decides is a 'party' to the case, or in other words has an interest in it. This may include the person's family or independent representative.
P	Purpose	Your report is in effect an expert witness statement and its purpose is to provide the judge with information to assist in making a judgement on whether the person concerned has the capacity to make their own decisions and also, where relevant, on the benefits or risks associated with a particular decision. Your report should be informed by your professional expertise in selecting and presenting evidence drawn from facts about the circumstances and research to back up your recommendations.

S	Self	Your report should reflect your professional view and judgement and you should be prepared to be questioned on the evidence you present and the basis for the judgements that you make. You may receive advice and guidance from the local authority solicitor and the report may need to be signed off by your line manager, but it must still represent your own professional judgement.
		(Baynes, 2017)

Report for a Mental Health Tribunal

C	Context	A Social Circumstances Report is required when a Mental Health Tribunal (formally the First-tier Tribunal Mental Health which is part of the Health, Education and Social Care Chamber) is considering discharge to the community after any order under the Mental Capacity Act 2005 arising from an appeal. Orders can be to detain someone for treatment or for assessment. Reports should include a Care Pathway Approach and/or an Aftercare Plan and contain a chronology. The Social Circumstances report is accompanied by a Clinician's Report and for in-patients a Nursing Report.
A	Audience	The primary audience is the tribunal panel which is chaired by a judge who normally sits alongside a mental health professional such as a psychiatrist and a lay person who has relevant knowledge or experience (Seymour and Seymour, 2011). Your report will also be read by the subject of the report and their legal representative and may be shared with the person's nearest relative or independent representative.
P	Purpose	Your report is in effect an expert witness statement and the purpose is to inform the tribunal of relevant history and present social circumstances that have a bearing on the hearing. It should provide all relevant information about the social context to which a person would be released to the community including risks and support. It will be informed by consultation with a number of people in addition to the detained person. These may include the person's family members, carer or advocate, community service providers such as housing, education or employment providers and health professionals. If a MAPPA (multi-agency public protection arrangements) team or meeting has been convened, they should also be consulted. Your report should be informed by your professional expertise in selecting and presenting evidence drawn from facts about the circumstances and research to back up your recommendations.
S	Self	Social Circumstances Reports must be completed by a community-based practitioner, who may be a social worker or a community nurse. Your report should reflect your professional view and judgement and you should be prepared to be questioned on the evidence you present and the basis for the judgements that you make.

Persuasive writing for court

The importance of using your professional judgement as a social worker was discussed in Chapter 8 and we return to this again now. In any report for court you are expected to use your own professional expertise to make a recommendation based on evidence.

As an expert witness the court will expect you to not only gather and collate relevant information but to use your experience and expertise to draw a conclusion upon which your recommendations are based. One way to think about making a case to the court is to apply the principles of persuasive, or rhetorical, writing.

Some linguists would argue that all writing is, to a degree, rhetorical (Bazerman, 1988; Prior, 1998). The concept of rhetoric is used in different ways, but here refers to communicating in order to persuade the reader. The discipline (for example social policy) and profession (for example social work) will have an influence on not only the content (what is written) but also how texts are written. You saw in Chapter 3 that essays require you to construct an argument, using your analysis of the evidence to reach a conclusion. The ways in which you construct your argument form a text which is rhetorical, or persuasive. In other words, your writing should persuade the reader to share or at least understand your conclusions. Rhetorical writing is also a feature of professional writing through using evidence to justify your professional judgement, expressed as recommendations. While the use of your professional judgement to provide recommendations based on evidence is a core element of much professional writing, for example assessment reports, it is a particularly important feature of reports written for court.

Persuasive writing then aims to persuade the audience or reader of a particular perspective or course of action based on evidence and argument. Katz (2018) suggests that the origins of rhetorical writing lie in the Classical Greek concepts of pathos, logos and ethos:

Pathos   Refers to the use of emotion to engage and persuade the reader.

Logos   Involves persuading the reader through logic and reasoning based on evidence and argument. Logos is also closely associated with the credibility of the writer.

Ethos   Refers to adapting the way in which you write in order to persuade a particular audience.

Ethos resonates with the concept of audience in CAPS, and there is also a relationship between logos and self, your credibility as an author. You will find further discussion of both argumentation (logos) and emotion (pathos) throughout this book, but here the focus is on the ways in which an awareness of pathos, logos and ethos can be helpful when writing a text this is intended to persuade the reader of a particular point view.

Activity 9.3

For this activity read the extracts from Chanice's report in Activity 9.2 again and as you read try to identify any of the features in the table below. You may also like to repeat this exercise with a report that you have written yourself.

Pathos	Logos	Ethos
Use of words or phrases that could be considered emotive in the context of: • describing events or observations • emphasising urgency or seriousness • stressing a recommendation • using direct words of others, such as service users, which contain emotive language	• Identification of the writer's status • Language which indicates the expertise of the writer • Reference to evidence language which indicates that an argument is being constructed • Professional recommendation/ view expressed	• Does the language used suggest who the intended reader (s) are? • Are complex or specialist words used including jargon or acronyms? Who would understand these terms? • Has language been used which would take account of a particular service user, such as a child, someone with a disability or who speaks English as a second or additional language? • Based on the language used, who do you think is the *primary* audience the writer is trying to convince or persuade?

Comment

This report extract does not include many directly emotive words and most of the language is explicitly not emotive. The report does include words such as 'illicit' rather than maybe 'illegal' and other phrases such as 'Brent has engaged with services on a superficial level', 'she leads a very chaotic and unstable lifestyle' and 'sporadic and inconsistent engagement', while being descriptive, also convey an emotive element. However, it is important to consider whether the use of specific words are descriptive or imply a judgement intended to have an emotive impact.

Logos is mostly evident in the processes that surround the court report itself. For example, the social worker completes the report as an expert witness. Authority as the writer is also granted in part from the use of language which references or suggests professional expertise, for example:

Chanice requires a stable, nurturing and safe environment where she will have opportunity to grow, develop and thrive.

and

Chanice is not of an age where she is able to express her likes and dislikes. She should therefore be provided the opportunity to experience different activities and explore appropriately to enable her to develop her sense of self.

Both of these claims are rooted in theory gained through professional training. A reference or source could be provided for them in the report, or alternatively a court may ask a social worker to substantiate these claims verbally in court.

Recommendations are also included in the report and these are written in the third person, which has the impact of distancing the writer from the recommendations. To illustrate, the report states that 'The local authority has considered . . .', 'There are no concerns regarding Carol's physical health . . .' and 'The local authority has considered the following . . .' By using such phrases rather than 'I have considered' or even 'It is my professional view that' the social worker clearly indicates the institutional status of the report and that they are writing on behalf of their agency. Baynes (2017) suggests that the court prefers social work reports to clearly be those of an independent expert witness, and if the social worker's professional view or recommendation differs from that of their employing authority this should be stated and a senior manager should provide additional evidence to support the agency recommendations.

The ethos of the writing indicates an intention to be accessible to the intended reader through the use of simple everyday language. There is some use of technical/specialist terms and a couple of abbreviations are used but in the main the report is written in simple, accessible language. Some words used do have a particular meaning in the context of social work, for example, 'developmental needs', 'emotional warmth', 'self-harming behaviours' and 'engagement', which would be understood by health and social care colleagues but perhaps less so by service users and perhaps the judge. There are also some terms which have a legal significance: 'Special Guardianship Order', 'Interim Child Arrangement Order' and 'parental capacity' may not be clear to all service users but will be well understood by the judge. The only abbreviation which may not be commonly understood is 'MAT' which refers to a 'multi-agency team'.

You may not have thought about reports as being persuasive, and may feel uncomfortable about the idea of your role as a social worker being to persuade others of a particular course of action. Thinking of a report as being persuasive does not imply that the author is being subjective, biased or manipulative. It does recognise that your role as a social worker is to:

- be clear and confident about your professional expertise
- collate and synthesise information, including gathering the views of the service user, family/carers and other professionals
- undertake an analysis drawing on your professional experience and knowledge (including theory, legislation and policy)
- arrive at a professional view which balances all parties' rights, responsibilities and risks
- provide clear recommendations which reflect complexity where it exists and acknowledge different perspectives.

It is this professional view that should guide the persuasive stance of the report and result in a recommendation. There may be times when a report might offer more than one possible course of action, or indeed no action at all, but in all cases the conclusion reached should be based on a well-argued and evidenced professional view.

Writing a persuasive document does raise ethical issues, primarily the power that the social worker has when compiling an assessment or review and capturing this in a report. As with all social work practice it is important that this power is recognised and managed ethically, rather than denying its existence. McDonald et al. suggest that *If used ethically, persuasive writing is not about trickery or manipulation but about targeting information for a client-centred result* (2015, p371). To achieve ethical persuasive writing the imbalances of power need to be recognised in order to allow all relevant voices to be represented. A persuasive report should not exclude the views of, for example, the service user or carer. There will be occasions where you are aware that the service user or a carer might disagree with your evaluation and recommendations. Such differences of view should be included openly, but it is the role of the social worker to weigh up all of the views and evidence in order to make a recommendation. This difficult work is an integral part of social work practice; the writing only reflects the practice through an articulation of the analysis and professional view offered.

Chapter summary

Writing for courts and tribunals raises considerable anxiety. In this chapter you have been introduced to some of the most common contexts in which you may be required to write a statement or report. As with all writing the details of how and what you should write depend on the context, purpose, who will be reading the report and your own role. In most cases you will be supported and advised by your line manager and often also a solicitor, so you will rarely be responsible for these important documents on your own. Applying CAPS will give you a good start in thinking about how to approach preparing written evidence for court but as part of understanding the context you will need to familiarise yourself with relevant guidance, which may include statutory directions, such as Practice Direction 22 within the Family Procedure Rules 2010. Perhaps most importantly you should keep in mind that the purpose of a written statement is to convey your professional judgement and recommendations to court, and this is based on your knowledge, experience and skills as a social work practitioner.

Further reading

CoramBAAF Adoption and Fostering Academy. At: https://corambaaf.org.uk/about (accessed 24 September 2020).

This online resource contains advice and guidance on all areas of adoption and fostering including writing reports. The site contains a template for the Prospective Foster Carer Report (Form F assessment).

Seymour, C and Seymour, R (2011) *Courtroom and Report Writing Skills for Social Workers.* London: Macmillan.

This is a very accessible book which provides a straightforward overview of the court system and advice on how to prepare reports for court in a range of contexts.

10

Therapeutic writing

Introduction

The focus so far has been on the product of writing, the final document process. The aim of both academic and professional writing is broadly to communicate something to the reader. In all of these contexts writing has great power. For student writers the outcome of assessment writing can result in pass or fail results, qualification or failure to qualify. In social work practice writing has the power to change lives in many ways from decisions about a child's life or removal of liberty for a vulnerable person through to the allocation or withdrawal of funding for care or services. In this chapter the focus is on the powerful impact that the *process* of writing can have and the ways in which this can be used in a variety of therapeutic contexts. Bolton suggests that:

> *Writing has been compared to fire – it can release energy, lead to catharsis and healing; it can be warming and comforting but it is also possible to be burned or even destroyed by it. The writing process should be treated with the same respect with which we treat fire – it is a valuable resource if properly harnessed.*

(Bolton et al., 2006, p19)

Some writing has value both in terms of its end product and the process of writing it. For example, in Chapter 4 you explored reflective writing which has an end product of being an assessed task, but the process of reflecting is also intended to deepen learning. For some writing the primary aim is for the process of writing to have some therapeutic, reflective or developmental impact. An understanding of how writing can be used therapeutically can have great value when working with service users but also in your own development as a practitioner. Therapeutic writing can be used in a wide range of contexts. It can be used with a wide range of ages and in both one to one-and-group contexts. I am interpreting 'writing' very broadly here to include diagrams, images, texts and combinations of these written forms.

How can writing be therapeutic?

The benefits of writing to express emotion have been recognised in a number of studies (Costa and Abreu, 2018; Bolton, 1999; Bolton et al., 2006). One study by Pennebaker and Beal (1986) examined the experiences of two groups, one of which was asked to write about upsetting experiences. The group writing about upsetting experiences found this difficult at the time, but when compared with the other group they showed an improvement in mood and well-being in the longer term. This study was undertaken in laboratory conditions and may not replicate experience in the real world. It is important to be aware that the emotional impact that some people may have in the longer term and to ensure that appropriate support is available (Costa and Abreu, 2018).

Writing in a variety of forms also has a well-recognised role in social work education and practice. The educational value of reflective writing has been explored in Chapter 4, but reflective writing can also have an important emotional impact on the writer which has the potential to have a therapeutic benefit. Writing has been used as a therapeutic tool in the context of work with a wide range of service users including older people, people with mental health needs and also children and young people. Some of the ways in which writing can be helpful are as follows:

- It can open up communication where service users need support to build trust or articulate feelings.
- It can be used in group contexts to express shared experiences or feelings.
- It can be a tool to explain difficult concepts or events in communication between a social worker and a service user.
- It can be a personal tool to express difficult feelings as part of a process of dealing with trauma.
- It can allow the expression of feelings and experiences through a mixture of words and images and also reality and fantasy.
- The writing could be in the form of a story, a letter, a poem or images with words.

Writing can have a therapeutic benefit for readers as well as writers, for example poetry therapy with mental health patients (Costa and Abreu, 2018). Poetry can have a significant power to connect and release emotion.

Activity 10.1

The following poem had a big impact on me when I first read it, and I still find it moving today. Read the poem yourself and write down some notes about what thoughts, memories or feelings it generates for you. Can you think of how it could be used with service users?

Holding on

Look here, my boy, I breast-fed you.
I burped you and I stayed up nights.
I played at monsters, taught you songs
extracted you from many fights,
explained the off-side rule to you
(which you now say I don't quite get)
and, yes, I may be old and odd –
but, please, do not ignore me yet.

I held your little hand along
the tops of walls for sev'ral years
and when you let go, wobbled, fell,

I kissed you better, dried your tears.
I taught you how to blow your nose,
to count to ten, to wash your kit
and overnight you see me as
some sad, outdated kind of twit.

Now, once again, at just fifteen
you suddenly let go of me.
You think you really cannot fall,
discounting the world's gravity.

Ah, let me hold your great big hand
another year, or two, or three.
My love, you do not know at all
how very hard the world can be.

© Lucy Berry (Reproduced with kind permission)

Comment

I came across this poem when my son was also 15 and it had great resonance with the mixed feelings I experienced as a parent – taking joy in the growing independence of a child mixed with the loss of my identity as a mother and being confronted with time passing as childhood fades and aging approaches. It also reminded me of the importance of interdependence in generations and the trust and negotiation that are needed

(Continued)

(Continued)

in families as they mature. I can't imagine an academic book or even prose, whether autobiographical or fiction, having the same impact. This poem could be used in teaching but also with parents, children or older people to help them to reflect on these experiences and emotions, either in a one-to-one session or, perhaps even more effectively, in a group session where the poem could stimulate discussion of parenting styles or reminiscence for older people. This approach was used by the Teens Out Loud project, a creative writing group for adolescents with HIV. The group used poetry reading alongside creative writing to reduce social isolation and encourage emotional personal growth (Fair et al., 2012).

The power of reading and writing expressive, reflective or creative texts, therefore, can be an important way to open up communication, particularly where strong emotions or difficult experiences are involved. This does not need to be in a formally therapeutic context and can include a wide range of techniques which might involve the use of drawing, creating writing/drawings collaboratively as well as talking about reading. Before looking at some examples of ways in which writing can be used therapeutically, complete the following activity which will give you an experience of expressive writing.

Activity 10.2

Writing exercises

For each of these writing exercises try to follow these 'rules':

1. Keep writing for the full time allotted – set a timer on your phone to check how long you have written for.
2. Keep your fingers moving and don't spend time thinking, if you get stuck write down the prompt again and try to pick up your thoughts again from there.
3. You are writing for yourself, so write whatever comes to mind and don't try to self-edit for a reader or to correct anything.
4. When you get to the end of the time given, put your writing aside and move onto the next exercise. You will return to read it later.
5. Write in the first person (I remember, I think, etc.).

First writing exercise

Time: 3 minutes

Prompt: My first memory of social work is . . .

Describe it as best as you are able using as many nice, juicy adjectives as you can. When you walked into a social work office for the first time how did it feel and what did you think? What did it look like? How did it smell? How did it sound? How did it feel? Who did you meet who made an impression on you and why?

Second writing exercise

Time: 5 minutes

Prompt: Who are you as a social worker?

1. Consider what strengths you have, what you are proud of, what you have accomplished. But also think about your *story* as a social worker.
2. What attracted you to be a social worker?
3. Who were you then?
4. Who are you now?

Third writing exercise

Time: 10 minutes

Prompt: If you were going to redesign social work how would it look?

1. What would you keep and what would you change?
2. How would changes impact on you being the kind of social worker you would like to be?

When you have completed all of the writing exercises set them aside for a while, go and make a drink or go for a walk, and when you return read them to yourself. Try not to be critical about presentation (spelling, grammar, layout) but focus on the feelings and memories that emerged from your writing. Reflect on the memories that this exercise has awakened and note down any ideas or raised awareness that the exercise has stimulated.

Comment

This kind of writing activity works very well when you can talk with someone to share your reflections, but people also find the quiet individual reflection and thinking time very helpful. Giving yourself permission to write freely, without feeling constrained to create a final product for someone to read, can allow some really deep reflection to take place which can result in both internal learning and the spark for conversations which are hard to generate in other ways. Adapting this kind of activity to different contexts can be a useful tool both as part of teaching/learning and in practice. The memories evoked can be particularly strong when you encourage the writer to recall places, smells, sounds and the sensation of touch, all of which can be associated with feelings.

This is just one way in which writing can be used to stimulate reflective conversations. Having had a small experience of expressive writing yourself, this chapter will now explore some other examples of how writing and drawing are used in social work.

Using rich pictures in family work

One of the techniques which I found very effective when working in a family centre was creating rich pictures in the form of ecomaps with families. Rich pictures provide *a way to explore, acknowledge and define a situation and express it through diagrams* and *to open discussion and come to a broad, shared understanding of a situation* (Stevens, 2016). Diagrams have been used for many years in social work in the form of genograms, ecomaps and life maps. All of these are in effect rich pictures as they are tools to aid thinking and communication about what are often complex systems and ideas.

The centre I worked in provided a preventative service for children and young people who had been excluded from school and also had identified complex family needs. We worked within a broadly systemic approach (Goodman and Trowler, 2012) and some higher risk families received family therapy (Holosko et al., 2013). Family sessions which were not formal family therapy involved completing assessments with the whole family so that the ways in which relationships were working as a system could be explored. This has the benefit of removing the focus from any one member of the family, frequently the child, as 'the problem'. Completing a family ecomap involves using a large sheet of paper, such as a flipchart, and working together to draw members of the family, significant others connected to the family (such as extended family, close friends, neighbours, teachers and employers). The relationships between people, including where they live, can be identified by adding lines, colours, placing people near or further from each other and adding text. All members of the family can be involved in writing and drawing, but importantly the worker can use the creating of the ecomap to encourage conversations about the family network. Creating an ecomap can be an enjoyable activity which family members of any age and ability can join in with, and it can be a way in which control is given to less powerful members of the family, for example by nominating them to draw or talk. For younger children play and toys can be introduced, for example small dolls, figures or Plasticine can be used to represent people or pets and photos of the final ecomap can be taken to keep a record of it. Using this activity I was often surprised at the information, feelings or views that family members expressed that had never been articulated before. As a result this was not only a rich tool for assessment but also provided a useful therapeutic tool.

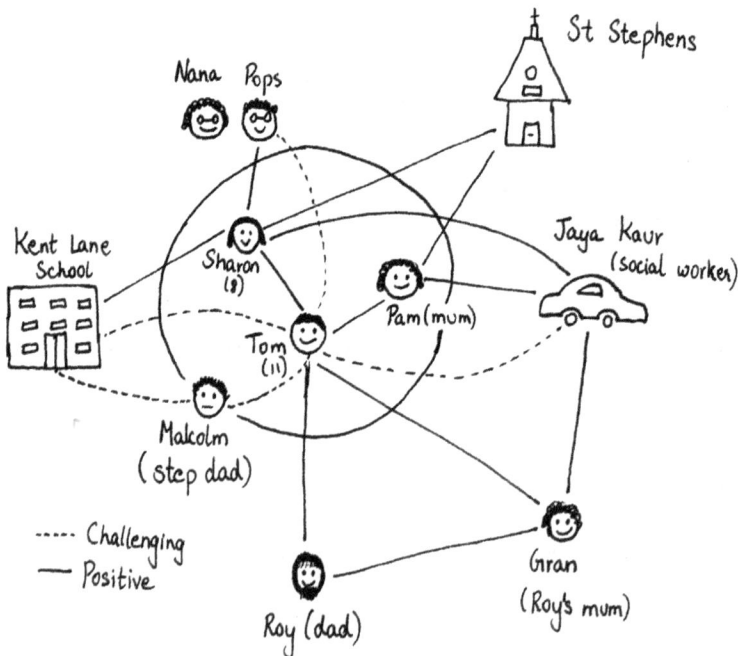

Figure 10.1 Use of diagrams with service users

There are many similar tools that can be used such as individual genograms and life maps. All share the use of diagrams created with service users during a purposeful conversation which might have be for the purpose of assessment, therapy or helping the service user to understand a complex story or sequence of events. What is important with all of these tools is to remember that the focus should be on the process of creating the diagram and the reflecting, thinking and conversations that take place while it is being created rather than on the final product.

Using letters in safeguarding work with children

Supporting children to disclose abuse is an extremely sensitive area of practice. Great care is needed in not breaching guidelines which are put in place to avoid putting evidence at risk. There are some circumstances, however, where writing can be a useful tool to help children to talk about experiences that are very difficult to verbalise. It is important to let children know that if they share information with you, verbally or in writing, which raises concerns over their safety you will need to share this with other people who can help protect them. The charity Childline suggest that writing a letter can be a good way for a child to ask for help, and they provide a template on their website (Figure 10.2).

Dear _____,

I'd like you to know something, but it's hard to talk about:

What I want to tell you is:

_____

It's been happening for:

_____

It's making me feel:

_____

Here's how I'd like you to help me after you've read this letter:

_____

If you have to tell someone what I've said, please try to talk to me about it first.

Thank you,

_____

Figure 10.2 Childline Conversation Starter template

Source: Childline: https://www.childline.org.uk/info-advice/bullying-abuse-safety/getting-help/asking-adult-help/ (accessed 24 September 2020; #Writesomeonealetter)

Writing will not be an easier way to open a conversation for all children, but for some it may provide a first step to sharing anxieties or frightening experiences. I co-led an adolescent girls group which included members who had already disclosed sexual abuse and also members who were referred due to emotional difficulties but had not disclosed any abuse. Creating posters, poems, stories and pictures both individually and as a group provided the girls with opportunities to express feelings and experiences without making full disclosures, which often emerged gradually over time as trust was developed. As with the rich pictures, it is the process of creating that is more important than the final product, both in terms of providing a way to express difficult feelings and offering a tentative step towards making a disclosure.

Expressive writing in mental health

Mental health is perhaps the area where expressive and creative writing has been used most extensively as a therapeutic tool (for example, Padfield et al., 2017; Peterkin and Prettyman, 2009; Costa and Abreu, 2018). One example is a self-directed treatment for mild to moderate post-traumatic stress disorder (PTSD) at Cardiff and Vale University Health Board Stress Service, based at the National Centre for Mental Health at Cardiff University, called 'Spring'. Spring delivers treatment through a guided digital application supported by counselling sessions with a psychologist. The approach is based on an eight-step programme, one of the most important elements of this involving the writing of a detailed, first-person present-tense account of the trauma that had been the trigger for the PTSD. Service users are then encouraged to read the letter repeatedly to effectively de-sensitise themselves to the events described. A later step involves writing a letter to a friend, imagining that this friend is you. The aim of this letter is to help service users gain an external perspective by providing support and also by challenging any feelings of guilt or shame lingering from the trauma (Lewis, 2011; Open University, 2020). The use of writing in this programme makes use of a number of techniques. It is based around the value of writing a detailed narration of an event to help the service user face memories which are perhaps being repressed. It then uses the process of reading and re-reading to de-sensitise the service user to the experience. The letter allows the service user to use reflection to step outside of their own experience and give themselves reassuring feedback as if from a caring third party. It is very important to recognise that this approach is supported through regular contact with a psychologist so that, as in the earlier examples, although the writing has a valuable therapeutic role it is used in combination with talking therapy. Also as with the previous examples in this chapter it is the process of writing and reading which is valuable rather than the final written piece itself.

Writing in supervision

Process recording was briefly introduced in Chapter 4 and involves writing a very detailed narrative based on observation of the encounter, including as much detail as the practitioner can recall. Process recording could be described as a form of professional 'therapy' with the aim of supporting practitioners to reflect critically and to take note of feelings and potentially subconscious responses which might provide useful insights into more effective practice. This includes what was said and communicated in other ways such as facial expression and body language, any observations about the environment and any actions that may not have been included as 'communication'. Importantly process recording should include the thoughts and feelings of the practitioner. Process recording should include the following:

- Factual information about everyone involved in the encounter (names, ages, relationships, roles, etc.).
- Objectives or purpose for the encounter.
- A detailed word-for-word description of what happened as well as the student can recall.
- A description of any action or nonverbal activity that occurred.
- The student's feelings and reactions to the service user and to the intervention as it took place. This requires the student to put in writing unspoken thoughts and reactions as the interview is going on (e.g. 'At this point I began to feel uneasy. I was a little frightened and wondered what to do next.')
- The student's observations and analytical thoughts regarding what has been happening during an interview (e.g. 'I wondered what would happen if I said such-and-such. I chose not to but I wondered whether I should have raised it', or 'Mrs S. said she felt happy but this seemed to contradict what she said earlier. I didn't think she looked very happy so I asked her to explain further.')
- A summary of the student's impressions. This is a summary of the student's analytical thinking about the entire interview.
- Future plans. Identification of unfinished business, identification of short and longer-term goals.
- Identification of questions for practice learning. This provides students with the opportunity to build upon their ability to become autonomous workers.

(Adapted from *Handbook for Student Social Work Recording*, Columbia University)

In Table 10.1 you can see an example of a short piece of process recording written by a newly qualified social worker based on a template with four headings. The first details the factual information in as much detail as the writer can remember. The second column is for immediate reflections and feelings and this is followed up by analysis, which may include thoughts, theory, knowledge or information that informed reflections either at the time or after the event. The final column is not written by the person who is reflecting on their practice but by their line manager, supervisor of assessor. The purpose of this column is to provide feedback but also prompts for further reflection in the context of a discussion of the process recording in supervision.

This kind of reflective recording is a valuable learning tool just through the process of writing it, but its value is greatest when shared and discussed within a supervision or mentoring relationship. With the declining popularity of psychoanalytic practice in the UK process recording is less common now, but it is still used elsewhere, for example in Australia (Karpetis, 2019) and the United States (Papell, 2015), and has great value when used by supervisors or mentors who have been trained in the approach. It is a very time-consuming activity and has, as a result, been unpopular with some students; nonetheless it offers a unique learning tool in social work education (Papell, 2015).

Table 10.1 Example of process recording

Content dialogue	Reflection and feelings	Analysis	Supervisor comments
I knock on the door, no reply but I can hear what sounds like glass breaking, furniture scraping on the floor and two voices shouting, one male and one female.	I had slight anxiety prior to this visit, I hoped it would be routine but if not I was worried about how to deal with the situation if Mrs T did not have an explanation or let me see Robert.	There had been a case review last week about Robert's attendance and I had some unsubstantiated concerns about the welfare of both children at the time. I had not met the partner but Mrs T had been co-operative.	Did you have a plan for if Mrs T invited you in and if she did not? Did you consider at this point whether you should withdraw and return with assistance?
After about 5 minutes of knocking Mrs T opens the door with the chain on, she appears pale and anxious, looking behind her several times. A female child (appears about three years old) is also visible, holding onto Mrs T's trousers.	My anxiety was increased by Mrs T's appearance the raised voices and slowness in answering the door and this was now around the safety of both children rather than just school attendance. I was already thinking about how I would respond if Mrs T did not answer or let me in.	It appeared that Mrs T did not want to allow me into the flat, but at this point I did not know why. There was no sign of Robert and I was more resolved that I probably needed to actually see Robert, I was relieved to see his sister but couldn't see enough of her to feel reassured. I was consciously aware of my duty to see the children to satisfy myself that they were safe. I was aware that although the reason for my visit was Robert's non school attendance, there was potential risk to his younger sister who was more vulnerable due to her age and the fact that she is pre-school and therefore not seen regularly by any professionals.	Was there anything specific about Mrs T or the little girls appearance that concerned you? Were there any visible signs of injury? Good that you remained aware of the need to see *both* children and that Robert's sister was potentially at more risk even though not the subject of the call
Me: Good morning, I am sorry to disturb you, I am the social worker from the children's team, we met at school last week. Would it be OK to come in for a quick chat about Robert (R)? Mrs T: I yeah, I think I remember, I am sorry this isn't a good time. My other half is just home from a night shift and needs to sleep. What is it about anyway? Me: I don't want to disturb you both, but I do need a quick word. We had a call from Robert's teacher, Mr Guy, this morning to let us know that Robert was not in school again. Is he here? Mrs T: Nah, he isn't here, he left for school this morning, I think he did. Look this really isn't a good time [the little girl is now crying and holding her arms up to be lifted, the chain is still on the door]	I was relieved once Mrs T opened the door and focused on being reassuring and professional. I felt relieved that I had at least made some contact and seen Robert's sister.	My focus was on ideally seeing both children, even if briefly, while maintaining the trust of Mrs T. I was keen to establish a working relationship allowing me to follow up with her at a later point if needed.	Good that you recognised the balance needed between seeing the children and maintaining co-operation with Mrs T

Content dialogue	Reflection and feelings	Analysis	Supervisor comments
Male voice shouting from inside the flat: Who the fxxx is that? Get rid of her! Just tell her to fxxx off! Robert is fine, I can hear him on that game of his as usual. Mrs T [sounding very anxious]: I need to go, I'll ring school OK?	I was aware of my anxiety increasing when I hear the tone of the man's voice. I knew this was not the children's father and that I knew nothing about him. I was also concerned now for Mrs T's welfare. I could feel my pulse racing as despite my anxiety I didn't want the situation to escalate or the door to be shut before I saw the children.	I was aware that the level of risk had potentially increased and that I may not gain entry. If this was the case I may need back up and I was thinking about how to respond if the door was shut. I was trying to recall any information about a partner but could not think of anything in the file or discussed at the recent meeting with school. I was focused on remaining calm but assertive.	Good to recognise at this point that you needed to seek some advice and support. You also needed to be able to access the information you were unsure about regarding the partner.
Me: I am sorry Mrs T, I really do need to talk to you and see Robert. It won't take long and we can maybe fix another time to talk properly, at my office or at school if that is easier? Mrs T: Look I will go and get Robert, he is here, he wasn't well this morning but he is fine. I will let you see him will you go and I will call you to make an appointment, OK?	When Mrs T said she would fetch Robert I relaxed slightly.	I was aware that by shutting the door rather than inviting me into the flat the likelihood of me seeing the children may have reduced.	Good response, well done.
[The door is slammed shut, I can hear indistinct shouting from inside and the noise of a child crying. I wait for several minutes and knock again when Mrs T does not return. I wait for 15 minutes, knocking and calling for Mrs T but the door is not opened. I put a note through the door explaining that I will return in half an hour.]	I felt a mixture of frustration, anxiety and relief. While I was concerned for the children and increased urgency of gaining entry, I also knew that at this point I needed some support. I felt frustrated with myself that maybe I could have handled the situation better.	The level of risk was potentially higher at this point, there was a potential that Mrs T was hiding something and that the children were at risk. I was equally aware, however, that her reluctance might be to avoid a confrontation with her partner. I was aware that I needed to discuss the situation with the duty manager and that I would potentially need to return with a colleague or the police, although I was unsure about whether the level of risk justified this?	I am glad you honestly acknowledged that you felt a degree of relief that you were starting to feel out of your depth and did not need to continue handling the situation without some support.

Chapter summary

In this chapter you have explored the ways in which writing can be used therapeutically. This has taken you beyond writing for academic purposes and documenting your professional work to providing a tool for helping service users to reflect, express their thoughts and feelings and deepen their understanding of complex experiences. We have also slightly stretched the usual understanding of 'writing' to incorporate drawings and diagrams in the form of rich pictures. These forms of expression, along with the use of creative forms such as stories and poems, can be an invaluable way of enriching your practice with service users with a wide range of communication needs and preferences.

Further reading

Bolton, G and Delderfield, R (2018) *Reflective Practice: Writing and Professional Development.* London: Sage.

This book provides a fascinating exploration of the ways in which writing can be used as a therapeutic and reflective tool. It includes exercises and activities, content on using e-portfolios and discussion of reflection as key employability skills. Gillie Bolton has published extensively in the area of therapeutic and reflective writing.

Gillam, T (2018) *Creativity, Wellbeing and Mental Health Practice.* London: Palgrave.

This is a practical, evidence-based book for students, practitioners and researchers in mental health nursing and related disciplines which explores the ways in which creativity, including writing, can contribute to mental health. Chapter 7 in particular addresses creative writing, literature and storytelling as therapeutic tools in mental health work.

Appendix 1

Professional capabilities framework

The 9 Domains

1. PROFESSIONALISM – Identify and behave as a professional social worker, committed to professional development.
2. VALUES AND ETHICS – Apply social work ethical principles and value to guide professional practices.
3. DIVERSITY AND EQUALITY – Recognise diversity and apply anti-discriminatory and anti-oppressive principles in practice.

4. RIGHTS, JUSTICE AND ECONOMIC WELL-BEING – Advance human rights and promote social justice and economic well-being.

5. KNOWLEDGE – Develop and apply relevant knowledge from social work practice and research, social sciences, law, other professional and relevant fields, and from the experience of people who use services.

6. CRITICAL REFLECTION AND ANALYSIS – Apply critical reflection and analysis to inform and provide a rationale for professional decision-making.

7. SKILLS AND INTERVENTIONS – Use judgement, knowledge and authority to intervene with individuals, families and communities to promote independence, provide support, prevent harm and enable progress.

8. CONTEXTS AND ORGANISATIONS – Engage with, inform and adapt to changing organisational contexts and the social and policy environments that shape practice. Operate effectively within and contribute to the development of organisations and services, including multi-agency and inter-professional settings.

9. PROFESSIONAL LEADERSHIP – Promote the profession and good social work practice. Take responsibility for the professional learning and development of others. Develop personal influence and be part of the collective leadership and impact of the profession.

(Published with kind permission of BASW. www.basw.co.uk)

Appendix 2

Subject benchmark for social work

5 Knowledge, understanding and skills

Subject knowledge and understanding

5.1 During their qualifying degree studies in social work, students acquire, critically evaluate, apply and integrate knowledge and understanding in the following five core areas of study.

5.2 Social work theory, which includes:

    i. critical explanations from social work theory and other subjects which contribute to the knowledge base of social work

    ii. an understanding of social work's rich and contested history from both a UK and comparative perspective

    iii. the relevance of sociological and applied psychological perspectives to understanding societal and structural influences on human behaviour at individual, group and community levels, and the relevance of sociological theorisation to a deeper understanding of adaptation and change

    iv. the relevance of psychological, physical and physiological perspectives to understanding human, personal and social development, well-being and risk

    v. social science theories explaining and exploring group and organisational behaviour

    vi. the range of theories and research-informed evidence that informs understanding of the child, adult, family or community and of the range of assessment and interventions which can be used

    vii. the theory, models and methods of assessment, factors underpinning the selection and testing of relevant information, knowledge and critical appraisal of relevant social science and other research and evaluation methodologies, and the evidence base for social work

    viii. the nature of analysis and professional judgement and the processes of risk assessment and decision-making, including the theory of risk-informed decisions and the balance of choice and control, rights and protection in decision-making

    ix. approaches, methods and theories of intervention in working with a diverse population within a wide range of settings, including factors guiding the choice and critical evaluation of these, and user-led perspectives.

5.3   Values and ethics, which include:

i.   the nature, historical evolution, political context and application of professional social work values, informed by national and international definitions and ethical statements, and their relation to personal values, identities, influences and ideologies

ii.   the ethical concepts of rights, responsibility, freedom, authority and power inherent in the practice of social workers as agents with statutory powers in different situations

iii.   aspects of philosophical ethics relevant to the understanding and resolution of value dilemmas and conflicts in both interpersonal and professional contexts

iv.   understanding of, and adherence to, the ethical foundations of empirical and conceptual research, as both consumers and producers of social science research

v.   the relationship between human rights enshrined in law and the moral and ethical rights determined theoretically, philosophically and by contemporary society

vi.   the complex relationships between justice, care and control in social welfare and the practical and ethical implications of these, including their expression in roles as statutory agents in diverse practice settings and in upholding the law in respect of challenging discrimination and inequalities

vii.   the conceptual links between codes defining ethical practice and the regulation of professional conduct

viii.   the professional and ethical management of potential conflicts generated by codes of practice held by different professional groups

ix.   the ethical management of professional dilemmas and conflicts in balancing the perspectives of individuals who need care and support and professional decision-making at points of risk, care and protection

x.   the constructive challenging of individuals and organisations where there may be conflicts with social work values, ethics and codes of practice

xi.   the professional responsibility to be open and honest if things go wrong (the duty of candour about own practice) and to act on concerns about poor or unlawful practice by any person or organisation

xii.   continuous professional development as a reflective, informed and skilled practitioner, including the constructive use of professional supervision.

5.4   Service users and carers, which include:

i.   the factors which contribute to the health and well-being of individuals, families and communities, including promoting dignity, choice and independence for people who need care and support

ii.   the underpinning perspectives that determine explanations of the characteristics and circumstances of people who need care and support, with critical evaluation drawing on research, practice experience and the experience and expertise of people who use services

iii.   the social and psychological processes associated with, for example, poverty, migration, unemployment, trauma, poor health, disability, lack of education and other sources of disadvantage and how they affect well-being, how they interact and may lead to marginalisation, isolation and exclusion, and demand for social work services

iv.   explanations of the links between the factors contributing to social differences and identities (for example, social class, gender, ethnic differences, age, sexuality and religious belief) and the structural consequences of inequality and differential need faced by service users

v.   the nature and function of social work in a diverse and increasingly global society (with particular reference to prejudice, interpersonal relations, discrimination, empowerment and anti-discriminatory practices).

5.5   The nature of social work practice, in the UK and more widely, which includes:

    i.   the place of theoretical perspectives and evidence from European and international research in assessment and decision-making processes

    ii. the integration of theoretical perspectives and evidence from European and international research into the design and implementation of effective social work intervention with a wide range of service users, carers and communities

    iii. the knowledge and skills which underpin effective practice, with a range of service-users and in a variety of settings

    iv. the processes that facilitate and support service user and citizen rights, choice, co-production, self-governance, well-being and independence

    v. the importance of interventions that promote social justice, human rights, social cohesion, collective responsibility and respect for diversity and that tackle inequalities

    vi. its delivery in a range of community-based and organisational settings spanning the statutory, voluntary and private sectors, and the changing nature of these service contexts

    vii. the factors and processes that facilitate effective interdisciplinary, inter-professional and interagency collaboration and partnership across a plurality of settings and disciplines

    viii. the importance of social work's contribution to intervention across service user groups, settings and levels in terms of the profession's focus on social justice, human rights, social cohesion, collective responsibility and respect for diversities

    ix. the processes of reflection and reflexivity as well as approaches for evaluating service and welfare outcomes for vulnerable people, and their significance for the development of practice and the practitioner.

5.6   The leadership, organisation and delivery of Social Work services, which includes:

    i.   the location of contemporary Social Work within historical, comparative and global perspectives, including in the devolved nations of the UK and wider European and international contexts

    ii. how the service delivery context is portrayed to service users, carers, families and communities

    iii. the changing demography and cultures of communities, including European and international contexts, in which social workers practise

    iv. the complex relationships between public, private, social and political philosophies, policies and priorities and the organisation and practice of social work, including the contested nature of these

    v. the issues and trends in modern public and social policy and their relationship to contemporary practice, service delivery and leadership in Social Work

    vi. the significance of legislative and legal frameworks and service delivery standards, including on core social work values and ethics in the delivery of services which support, enable and empower

    vii. the current range and appropriateness of statutory, voluntary and private agencies providing services and the organisational systems inherent within these

    viii. development of new ways of working and delivery, for example the development of social enterprises, integrated multi-professional teams and independent Social Work provision

    ix. the significance of professional and organisational relationships with other related services, including housing, health, education, police, employment, fire, income maintenance and criminal justice

  x.   the importance and complexities of the way agencies work together to provide
       care, the relationships between agency policies, legal requirements and profes-
       sional boundaries in shaping the nature of services provided in integrated and
       interdisciplinary contexts
  xi.   the contribution of different approaches to management and leadership within dif-
       ferent settings, and the impact on professional practice and on quality of care
       management and leadership in public and human services
 xii.   the development of person-centred services, personalised care, individual budgets
       and direct payments all focusing upon the human and legal rights of the service
       user for control, power and self determination
 xiii.   the implications of modern information and communications technology for both
       the provision and receipt of services, use of technologically enabled support and
       the use of social media as a process and forum for vulnerable people, families and
       communities, and communities of professional practice.

Subject-specific skills and other skills

5.7   The range of skills required by a qualified social worker reflect the complex and demand-
      ing context in which they work. Many of these skills may be of value in many situations,
      for example, analytical thinking, building relationships, working as a member of an
      organisation, intervention, evaluation, and reflection. What defines the specific nature of
      these skills as developed by social work students is:

  i.   the context in which they are applied and assessed (for example communication
       skills in practice with people with sensory impairments or assessment skills in an
       inter-professional setting)
  ii.   the relative weighting given to such skills within social work practice (for example,
       the central importance of problem-solving skills within complex human situations)
  iii.   the specific purpose of skill development (for example, the acquisition of research
       skills in order to build a repertoire of research-based practice)
  iv.   a requirement to integrate a range of skills (that is, not simply to demonstrate these
       in an isolated and incremental manner).

5.8   All social work graduates demonstrate the ability to reflect on and learn from the exercise
      of their skills, in order to build their professional identity. They understand the significance
      of the concepts of continuing professional development and lifelong learning, and accept
      responsibility for their own continuing development.
5.9   Social work students acquire and integrate skills in the following five core areas.

Problem-solving skills

5.10   These are subdivided into four areas.
5.11   Managing problem-solving activities: graduates in social work are able to:

  i.   think logically, systematically, creatively, critically and reflectively, in order to carry
       out a holistic assessment
  ii.   apply ethical principles and practices critically in planning problem-solving activities
  iii.   plan a sequence of actions to achieve specified objectives, making use of research,
       theory and other forms of evidence
  iv.   manage processes of change, drawing on research, theory and other forms of evidence.

5.12   Gathering information: graduates in social work are able to:

    i.   demonstrate persistence in gathering information from a wide range of sources and using a variety of methods, for a range of purposes. These methods include electronic searches, reviews of relevant literature, policy and procedures, face-to-face interviews, and written and telephone contact with individuals and groups

    ii. take into account differences of viewpoint in gathering information and critically assess the reliability and relevance of the information gathered

   iii. assimilate and disseminate relevant information in reports and case records.

5.13   Analysis and synthesis: graduates in social work are able to analyse and synthesise knowledge gathered for problem-solving purposes, in order to:

    i.   assess human situations, taking into account a variety of factors (including the views of participants, theoretical concepts, research evidence, legislation and organisational policies and procedures)

    ii. analyse and synthesise information gathered, weighing competing evidence and modifying their viewpoint in the light of new information, then relate this information to a particular task, situation or problem

   iii. balance specific factors relevant to social work practice (such as risk, rights, cultural differences and language needs and preferences, responsibilities to protect vulnerable individuals and legal obligations)

   iv. assess the merits of contrasting theories, explanations, research, policies and procedures and use the information to develop and sustain reasoned arguments

    v. employ a critical understanding of factors that support or inhibit problem-solving including societal, organisational and community issues as well as individual relationships

   vi. critically analyse and take account of the impact of inequality and discrimination in working with people who use social work services.

5.14   Intervention and evaluation: graduates in social work are able to use their knowledge of a range of interventions and evaluation processes creatively and selectively to:

    i.   build and sustain purposeful relationships with people and organisations in communities and inter-professional contexts

    ii. make decisions based on evidence, set goals and construct specific plans to achieve outcomes, taking into account relevant information including ethical guidelines

   iii. negotiate goals and plans with others, analysing and addressing in a creative and flexible manner individual, cultural and structural impediments to change

   iv. implement plans through a variety of systematic processes that include working in partnership

    v. practice in a manner that promotes well-being, protects safety and resolves conflict

   vi. act as a navigator, advocate and support to assist people who need care and support to take decisions and access services

  vii. manage the complex dynamics of dependency and, in some settings, provide direct care and personal support to assist people in their everyday lives

 viii. meet deadlines and comply with external requirements of a task

   ix. plan, implement and critically monitor and review processes and outcomes

    x. bring work to an effective conclusion, taking into account the implications for all involved

   xi. use and evaluate methods of intervention critically and reflectively.

Communication skills

5.15   Graduates in social work are able to communicate clearly, sensitively and effectively (using appropriate methods which may include working with interpreters) with individuals and groups of different ages and abilities in a range of formal and informal situations, in order to:

    i.   engage individuals and organisations, who may be unwilling, by verbal, paper-based and electronic means to achieve a range of objectives, including changing behaviour

    ii.   use verbal and non-verbal cues to guide and inform conversations and interpretation of information

    iii.   negotiate and where necessary redefine the purpose of interactions with individuals and organisations and the boundaries of their involvement

    iv.   listen actively and empathetically to others, taking into account their specific needs and life experiences

    v.   engage appropriately with the life experiences of service users, to understand accurately their viewpoint, overcome personal prejudices and respond appropriately to a range of complex personal and interpersonal situations

    vi.   make evidence-informed arguments drawing from theory, research and practice wisdom including the viewpoints of service users and/or others

    vii.   write accurately and clearly in styles adapted to the audience, purpose and context of the communication

    viii.   use advocacy skills to promote others' rights, interests and needs

    ix.   present conclusions verbally and on paper, in a structured form, appropriate to the audience for which these have been prepared

    x.   make effective preparation for, and lead, meetings in a productive way.

Skills in working with others

5.16   Graduates in social work are able to build relationships and work effectively with others, in order to:

    i.   involve users of social work services in ways that increase their resources, capacity and power to influence factors affecting their lives

    ii.   engage service users and carers and wider community networks in active consultation

    iii.   respect and manage differences such as organisational and professional boundaries and differences of identity and/or language

    iv.   develop effective helping relationships and partnerships that facilitate change for individuals, groups and organisations while maintaining appropriate personal and professional boundaries

    v.   demonstrate interpersonal skills and emotional intelligence that creates and develops relationships based on openness, transparency and empathy

    vi.   increase social justice by identifying and responding to prejudice, institutional discrimination and structural inequality

    vii.   operate within a framework of multiple accountability (for example, to agencies, the public, service users, carers and others)

    viii.   observe the limits of professional and organisational responsibility, using supervision appropriately and referring to others when required

    ix.   provide reasoned, informed arguments to challenge others as necessary, in ways that are most likely to produce positive outcomes.

Skills in personal and professional development

5.17   Graduates in social work are able to:

   i.   work at all times in accordance with codes of professional conduct and ethics

   ii. advance their own learning and understanding with a degree of independence and use supervision as a tool to aid professional development

   iii. develop their professional identity, recognise their own professional limitations and accountability, and know how and when to seek advice from a range of sources including professional supervision

   iv. use support networks and professional supervision to manage uncertainty, change and stress in work situations while maintaining resilience in self and others

   v. handle conflict between others and internally when personal views may conflict with a course of action necessitated by the social work role

   vi. provide reasoned, informed arguments to challenge unacceptable practices in a responsible manner and raise concerns about wrongdoing in the workplace

   vii. be open and honest with people if things go wrong

   viii. understand the difference between theory, research, evidence and expertise and the role of professional judgement.

Use of technology and numerical skills

5.18   Graduates in social work are able to use information and communication technology effectively and appropriately for:

   i.   professional communication, data storage and retrieval and information searching

   ii. accessing and assimilating information to inform working with people who use services

   iii. data analysis to enable effective use of research in practice

   iv. enhancing skills in problem-solving

   v. applying numerical skills to financial and budgetary responsibilities

   vi. understanding the social impact of technology, including the constraints of confidentiality and an awareness of the impact of the 'digital divide'.

References

Advance HE (2010) *Writing Learning Outcomes*. At https://www.advance-he.ac.uk/knowledge-hub/writing-learning-outcomes (accessed 30 September 2019).

Balkow, M and Lillis, T (2019) *Social Work Writing and Bureaucracy: A Tale in Two Voices*: A Discussion Paper from the Centre for Welfare Reform. Centre for Welfare Reform. At https://www.centreforwelfarereform.org/library/social-work-writing-and-bureaucracy.html (accessed 30 March 2020).

Baynes, P (2017) *Social Work Practice in Family Court*. Dartington: Research in Practice. At https://www.researchinpractice.org.uk/children/content-pages/videos/social-work-practice-in-family-court/ (accessed 6 June 2020).

Baynham, M (2000) Academic writing in new and emergent discipline areas. In M Lea and B Stierer (eds), *Student Writing in Higher Education: New Contexts*. Buckingham: Open University Press, pp. 17–31.

Bazerman, C (1988) *Shaping Written Knowledge: The Genre and Activity of the Experimental Article in Science*. Madison, WI: University of Wisconsin Press.

Blamires, K (2015) A summary of government initiatives relating to employment for people with learning disabilities in England. *Tizard Learning Disability Review*, 20(3): 151–65.

Bolton, G (1999) *The Therapeutic Potential of Creative Writing: Writing Myself*. London: Jessica Kingsley.

Bolton, G and Delderfield, R (2018) *Reflective Practice: Writing and Professional Development*. London: Sage.

Bolton, G, Field, V and Thompson, K (2006) *Writing Works: A Resource Handbook for Therapeutic Writing Workshops and Activities*. London: Jessica Kingsley.

Bottomley, J, Cartney, P and Pryjmachuk, S (2018) *Studying for Your Social Work Degree*, Critical Study Skills. St Albans: Critical Publishing.

Boud, D (1999) Avoiding the traps: seeking good practice in the use of self assessment and reflection in professional courses. *Social Work Education*, 18(2), pp. 121–32.

Bowlby, J and Institute of Psycho-Analysis (1982) *Attachment*, Vol. 1, 2nd edn. London: Hogarth Press and Institute of Psycho-Analysis.

British Association of Social Work (2018) *Professional Capabilities Framework*. Available at: https://www.basw.co.uk/professsional-development/professional-capabilities-framework-pdf (accessed 25 November 2020).

Bruner, J (1957) On perceptual readiness. *Psychological Review*, 64: 123–52.

Butler-Sloss, E (1988) *Report of the Inquiry into Child Abuse in Cleveland*. London: HMSO.

Care Act 2014 (England and Wales)

Care Inspectorate (2017) *Practice Guide to Chronologies: A Care Inspectorate Guide*, revising and replacing Social Work Inspection Agency (2010) *Practice Guide: Chronologies*.

Care Quality Commission (2017) *The State of Adult Social Care Services 2014 to 2017. Findings from CQC's Initial Programme of Comprehensive Inspections in Adult Social Care*. Available at: http://www.cqc.org.uk/sites/default/files/20170703_ASC_end_of_programme_FINAL2.pdf (accessed 10 February 2020).

Chelune, GJ (1979) *Self-disclosure: Origins, Patterns and Implications of Openness in Interpersonal Relationships*. San Francisco: Jossey-Bass.

Childline (2020) Available at https://www.childline.org.uk/info-advice/bullying-abuse-safety/getting-help/asking-adult-help/#Writesomeonealetter (accessed 11 June 2020).

Children and Families Act 2014 (England and Wales)

Coffin, C and Hewings, A (2003) Writing for different disciplines. In C Coffin, M Curry, S Goodman, A Hewings, TM Lillis and J Swann, *Teaching Academic Writing: A Toolkit for Higher Education*. London: Routledge.

Columbia State University. *Handbook for Student Social Work Recording*. Available at: https://socialwork.columbia.edu/wp-content/uploads/2015/06/Process_Recordings_Handbook1.pdf (accessed 2 January 2020).

Community Care (2019) 60% of social workers have work disrupted every week by case management system. At: https://www.communitycare.co.uk/2019/06/07/60-social-workers-work-disrupted-every-week-case-management-system/ (accessed 11 February 2020).

Costa, AC and Abreu, MV (2018) A escrita expressiva e criativa no contexto terapêutico: dos diferentes conceitos ao desenvolvimento de programas de escrita terapêutica. *Psychologica*, 1(61), pp. 69–86.

Courts and Tribunals Judiciary (2020) Available at: https://www.judiciary.uk/related-offices-and-bodies/advisory-bodies/fjc/guidance (accessed 24 September 2020).

Crème, P and Lea, M (2008) *Writing at University: A Guide for Students*. Maidenhead: McGraw-Hill/Open University Press.

Data Protection Act 1998. At: http://www.legislation.gov.uk/ukpga/1998/29/introduction/enacted?view=extent (accessed 11 February 2020).

Department for Children, Schools and Families and Department of Health (2009) *Building a Safe and Confident Future: Implementing the Recommendations of the Social Work Task Force*. London: HMSO.

Department of Education (2010) *Haringey Local Safeguarding Children Board Serious Case Review 'Child A'*. London: HMSO.

Department of Education (2011) *The Munro Review of Child Protection: Final Report – Child Centred System*. London: HMSO.

Department of Health (2001) *Valuing People: A New Strategy for Learning Disability for the 21st Century*, Cm 5086.

Department of Health (2007) *Putting People first*. Available at: http://www.cpa.org.uk/cpa/putting_people_first.pdf (accessed 25 November 2020).

Department of Health (2009) *Building a Safe and Confident Future: The Final Report of the Social Work Task Force*. London: HMSO.

DoE, DoH & SC Statutory Guidance (2014) *SEND Code of Practice: 0 to 25 years Guidance on the Special Educational Needs and Disability (SEND) System for Children and Young People Aged 0 to 25, from 1 September 2014*. At: https://www.gov.uk/government/publications/send-code-of-practice-0-to-25 (accessed 20 October 2020).

Downs, C and Craft, A (1996) Sexuality and profound and multiple impairment. *Tizard Learning Disability Review*, 1(4): 17–22.

Duncan-Daston, R and Schneller, D (2016) Teaching pragmatic psychodynamic psychotherapy to graduate social work students. *Journal of Teaching in Social Work*, 36(2): 176–96.

Dyke, C (2019) *Writing Analytical Assessments*. St Alban's: Critical Publishing.

Eraut, M (1994) *Developing Professional Knowledge and Competence*. London: Falmer.

Fair, CD, Connor, L, Albright, J, Wise, E and Jones, K (2012) '"I'm positive, I have something to say": assessing the impact of a creative writing group for adolescents living with HIV', *Arts in Psychotherapy*, 39: 383–9.

Family Procedure Rules Part 22 (2010) At: https://www.justice.gov.uk/courts/procedure-rules/family/parts/part_22 (accessed 11 September 2020).

Garcia-Maza, G, Lillis, T and Rai, L (2010) *Action Research Project on Case Notes Recording. Final Project Report*. Open University/Derbyshire County Council.

Getting It Right for Every Child (2012) *GIRFEC Briefing for Practitioners No. 8: Single Agency and Integrated Chronologies*. Scottish Government.

Gibbs, G (1988) *Learning by Doing*. Oxford: Oxford Polytechnic Further Education Unit.

Goffman, E (1969) *The Presentation of Self in Everyday Life*. London: Penguin.

Goodman, S and Trowler, I (2012) *Social Work Reclaimed: Innovative Frameworks for Child and Family Social Work Practice*. London: Jessica Kingsley.

Hamilton, R (2018) Work-based learning in social work education: the challenges and opportunities for the identities of work-based learners on university-based programs, *Social Work Education*.

Hardy, R. (2018) Why a chronology should be the first thing you do in an assessment, *Community Care*. At https://www.communitycare.co.uk/2018/08/15/chronology-first-thing-assessment/ (accessed 11 February 2020).

Hemm, C, Dagnan, D and Meyer, TD (2018) Social anxiety and parental overprotection in young adults with and without intellectual disabilities. *Journal of Applied Research in Intellectual Disabilities (JARID)*, 31(3): 360–8.

Heslop, P and Hebron, C (eds) (2020) *Promoting the Health and Well-Being of People with Learning Disabilities*. London: Springer.

Higher Education Authority (2019) *Learning Objectives and outcomes*. Available at https://www.heacademy.ac.uk/knowledge-hub/learning-objectives-and-outcomes (accessed 4 February 2019).

Holosko, MJ, Dulmus, CN and Sowers, KM (2013) *Social Work Practice with Individuals and Families: Evidence-Informed Assessments and Interventions*. Hoboken, NJ: John Wiley & Sons.

Horner, B and Lu, MZ (eds) (1999) *Representing the 'Other'. Basic Writers and the Teaching of Basic Writing*. Urbana, IL: National Council for Teachers of English.

Ivanič, R (1998) *Writing and Identity: The Discoursal Construction of Identity in Academic Writing*. Amsterdam: John Benjamins.

Jackson, D (2017) Challenges and strategies for assessing student workplace performance during work-integrated learning, *Assessment and Evaluation in Higher Education* 43(4): 555–70.

Judiciary UK (2013) At: https://www.judiciary.uk/wp-content/uploads/JCO/Documents/Practice+Directions/Tribunals/statements-in-mental-health-cases-hesc-28102013.pdf (accessed 20 August 2020).

Karpetis, G (2019) In-depth learning in field education: evaluating the effectiveness of process recording. *Journal of Social Work Practice*, 33(1): 95–107.

Katz, L (2018) *Critical Thinking and Persuasive Writing for Postgraduates*. London: Palgrave.

Kingsley, EP and Walker-Hirsch, L (2007) A parent's perspective: supporting challenges and strategies. In L Walker-Hirsch (ed.) *The Facts of Life and More . . . Sexuality and Intimacy for People with Intellectual Disabilities*. MD: Paul H. Brookes, pp.75–93.

Kolb, D (1970) *Learning in Groups*. London: Croom Helm.

Laming, WH (2003) *The Victoria Climbié inquiry: Report of an Inquiry by Lord Laming*, Cm 5730. London: TSO.

Lea, M and Stierer, B (eds) (2000) *Student Writing in Higher Education: New Contexts*. Buckingham: SRHE & Open University Press.

Lea, M and Street, B (1998) Student writing in higher education: an academic literacies approach. *Studies in Higher Education*, 23(2): 157–72.

Ledger, S, Townson, L with Docherty, D (2014) *Sexuality and Relationships in the Lives of People with Intellectual Disabilities: Standing in My Shoes*. Jessica Kingsley.

Leedham, M, Lillis, T and Twiner, A (2020) Exploring the core preoccupation of social work writing: A corpus-assisted discourse study. *Journal of Corpora and Discourse Studies* 2(1): 1–30.

Legislation.gov.uk. 2017. Children Act 1989. At: http://www.legislation.gov.uk/ukpga/1989/41/section/17 (accessed 16 June 2020).

Lewis, C (2011) *Phase I Development of a Guided Self Help (GSH) Programme for the Treatment of Mild to Moderate Post Traumatic Stress Disorder (PTSD)*. PhD Thesis, Cardiff University.

Lillis, T (1997) New voices in academia? The regulative nature of academic writing conventions. *Linguistics and Education*, 11(3): 182–99.

Lillis, T (2001) *Student Writing Access, Regulation and Desire*. London: Routledge.

Lillis, T (2010) *New Voices in Academia? The Regulative Nature of Academic Writing Conventions* (accessed September 2012), pp. 37–41.

Lillis, T (2017) Imagined, prescribed and actual text trajectories: the "problem" with case notes in contemporary social work. *Text and Talk*, 37(4): 485–508.

Lillis, T and Tuck, J (2016) Academic literacies: a critical lens on writing and reading in the academy. In K Hyland and P Shaw (eds) *The Routledge Handbook of English for Academic Purposes*, Routledge Handbooks. London: Routledge, pp. 30–43.

Lillis, T and Turner, J (2001) Student writing in higher education: contemporary confusion, traditional concerns. *Teaching in Higher Education*, 6(1): 57–68.

Lillis, T, Leedham, M and Twiner, A (2017) "If it's not written down it didn't happen": contemporary social work as a writing intensive profession, *Journal of Applied Linguistics and Professional Practice*, 14(1): 29–52.

Lillis, T, Leedham, M and Twiner, A (2020) Time, the written record and professional practice: the case of contemporary social work. *Written Communication*, 37(4): 431–86.

Lillis, T and Rai, L (2011) A case study of research-based collaboration around writing in social work. *Across the disciplines*, 8(3).

Lyons, K (1999) *International Social Work: Themes and Perspectives*. Farnham: Ashgate.

Lyons, K (2016) *International Social Work: Themes and Perspectives*. London: Routledge.

McCarthy, M. (1998) Whose body is it anyway? Pressures and control for women with learning disabilities. *Disability and Society*, 13(4): 557–74.

McDonald, D, Boddy, J, O'Callaghan, K and Chester, P (2015) Ethical *Professional Writing in Social Work and Human Services, Ethics and Social Welfare*, 9(4): 359–74.

Mellanby, J and Theobald, K (2014) *Education and Learning: An Evidence-Based Approach*. John Wiley & Sons.

Mencap (n.d.) *Transition into Adult Services. After Education or Training – What Next? See What Options There Are and How Your or Your Child's Services Will Change*. Available at: https://www.mencap.org.uk/advice-and-support/children-and-young-people/transition-adult-services (accessed 20 October 2020).

Mencap (2019) *What Is a Learning Disability?* At: www.mencap.org.uk.

Middleton, R. (2017) Critical reflection: the struggle of a practice developer. *International Practice Development Journal*, 7(1): 4-1-4-6.

Mullen, EJ, Bellamy, JL and Bledsoe, SE (2008) *Limits of Evidence in Evidence-Based Policy and Practice in Evidence Based and Knowledge Based Social Work: Research Methods and Approaches in Social Work Research*, ed. Inge M. Bryderup. Aarhus: Universitetsforlag,

Musson, P (2017) *Making Sense of Theory and Its Application to Social Work Practice*. St Albans: Critical Publishing.

Mullen, EJ, Bledsoe, SE and Bellamy, JL (2008) Implementing evidence-based social work practice. *Research on Social Work Practice*, 18(4): 325–38.

National Institute for Health and Care Excellence (NICE) (2016) Overarching principles. In *Transition from Children's to Adults' Services for Young People Using Health or Social Care Services*. At: www.nice.org.uk.

NHS (2019) *Assessing Capacity*. At: www.nhs.uk.

Northern Ireland Social Care Council (2019) *The Standards of Conduct and Practice for Social Workers*. Belfast: NSCC.

Open University (2014) *Advanced Evaluation Using PROMPT*. At: http://www.open.ac.uk/library-services/documents/advanced-evaluation-using-prompt.pdf (accessed 20 October 2020).

Open University (2020) *Accessing Mental Health in Wales: Introduction to Health and Social Care*, K102. At: https://learn2.open.ac.uk/mod/oucontent/view.php?id=1587830&section=3 <accessed 11 June 2020).

Open University (2020) Risk and addiction. In *Introducing Health and Social Care.* At: https://learn2.open.ac.uk/mod/oucontent/view.php?id=1511665&section=6 (accessed 20 October 2020).

Open University (2020) *Understanding Heath and Social Care.* Available at: https://learn2.open.ac.uk/mod/oucontent/view.php?id=1511665&section=6 (accessed 19 October 2020).

Padfield, B, Tominey, R and Matthews, L (2017) Therapeutic writing groups in specialist inpatient eating disorder treatment, *Journal for Specialists in Group Work*, 42(4): 316–37.

Papell, CP (2015) Process recording revisited: an essay on an educational artifact as a cognitive exercise. *Social Work with Groups*, 38: 3–4, 345–57.

Parker, J (2010) *Effective Practice Learning in Social Work*, 2nd edn. Exeter: Learning Matters.

Pennebaker, J W and Beal, SK (1986) Confronting a traumatic event: toward an understanding of inhibition and disease. *Journal of Abnormal Psychology*, 95: 274–81.

Peterkin, AD and Prettyman, AA (2009) Finding a voice: revisiting the history of therapeutic writing. *Medical Humanities*, 35(2): 80–8.

Prior, P (1998) *Writing/Disciplinarity: A Sociohistoric Account of Literate Activity in the Academy.* London: Lawrence Erlbaum Associates.

Quality Assurance Agency (2013) *UK Quality Code for Higher Education 2013–18.* Available at: https//www.qaa.ac.uk/quality-code/UK-Quality-code-for-Higher-Education-2013-18 (accessed 25 November 2020).

Quality Assurance Agency (2019) *Subject Benchmark Statement: Social Work.* Available at: https://www.qaa.ac.uk/docs/qaa/subject-benchmark-statements/subjects-benchmark-statement-social-work.pdf (accessed 25 November 2020).

Rai, L (2004) Exploring literacy in social work education: a social practices approach to student writing. *Social Work Education*, 23(2): 149–62. At: http://oro.open.ac.uk/913/.

Rai, L (2006) Owning (up to) reflective writing in social work education. *Social Work Education*, 25(8): 785–97. At: http://oro.open.ac.uk/22062/.

Rai, L (2008) *Student Writing in Social Work Education.* Open University. At: http://oro.open.ac.uk/25820/.

Rai, L. (2012) Responding to emotion in practice-based writing. *Higher Education*, 64(2), pp. 267–84.

Rai, L (2014) *Effective Writing for Social Work: Making a Difference.* Bristol: Policy Press.

Rai, L and Lillis, T (2011) A case study of research-based collaboration around writing in social work. *Across the Disciplines*, 8(3).

Rai, L and Lillis, T (2013) 'Getting it write' in social work: exploring the value of writing in academia to writing for professional practice. *Teaching in Higher Education*, September, pp. 1–13.

Reed, S (2015) *Successful Professional Portfolios for Nurses*, 2nd edn. London: Sage.

Ryding, J and Wernersson, I (2019) The role of reflection in family support social work and its possible promotion by a research-supported model. *Journal of Evidence-Based Social Work*, 16(3): 322–45.

Schön, D (1983) *The Reflective Practitioner: How Professionals Think in Action.* London: Temple Smith.

Schön, D (1989) *Educating the Reflective Practitioner: Towards a New Design for Teaching and Learning in the Professions.* San Francisco: Jossey-Bass.

SCIE. Last updated 2019. At: https://www.scie.org.uk/social-work/recording.

SCIE (2016) *Euphemistic Language in Reports and Written Records*, Practice Issues from Serious Case Reviews 13. At: https://www.scie.org.uk/safeguarding/children/case-reviews/learning-from-case-reviews/13.asp (accessed 20 October 2020).

SCIE Social Work Recording. At: https://www.scie.org.uk/social-work/recording (accessed 23 March 2020).

Scottish Government (2012) *Getting it Right for Every Child: GIRFEC Briefing for Practioners No. 8: Single Agency and Integrated Chronologies.* Scottish Government.

Scottish Social Services Council (2016) *Codes of Practice for Social Service Workers and Employers.* Edinburgh: SSSC.

Seebohm Committee (1968) *Report of the Committee on Local Authority and Allied Personal Social Services*, Cmnd 3703. London: HMSO.

Sentencing Council (2019) Sentencing Offenders with Mental Health Conditions or Disorders – Consultation Document. At: https://www.sentencingcouncil.org.uk/offences/magistrates-court/item/sentencing-offenders-with-mental-health-conditions-or-disorders-for-consultation-only/#annexc (accessed 21 April 2020).

Seymour, C and Seymour, R (2011) *Courtroom and Report Writing for Social Workers*. Exeter: Learning Matters.

Social Care Institute for Excellence (2020) *Social Work Recording*. At: https://www.scie.org.uk/social-work/recording?gclid=Cj0KCQiAm4TyBRDgARIsAOU75splbEdRWKXlCItkcvMCAas4tlo_H9qGYIV1WjxRAGEA4GbhSnUlLpkaAqShEALw_wcB (accessed 10 February 2020).

Social Care Wales (2019) *The Social Worker: Practice Guidance for Social Workers Registered with Social Care Wales*. Cardiff: SCW.

Social Work England (2019) *Professional Standards*. London: SWE. At: https://www.social-workengland.org.uk/standards/professional-standards/ (accessed 5 April 2020).

Social Work England. At: https://socialworkengland.org.uk/.

Social Work Reform Board (2010) *Building a Safe and Confident Future: One Year On*. London: HMSO.

Solomon, P and Draine, J (2010) An overview of quantitative research methods. In BA Thyer (eds), *The Handbook of Social Work Research Methods*, 2nd edn. London: Sage.

Stevens, K (2016) *Rich Pictures*. At: https://www.betterevaluation.org/en/evaluation-options/rich-pictures (accessed 11 June 2020).

Street, B (1984) *Literacy in Theory and Practice*. Cambridge: Cambridge University Press.

Thompson, N (2017) *Theorizing Practice*, 2nd edn. London: Palgrave.

Towers, C (2013) *Thinking Ahead: A Planning Guide for Families*. London: Foundation for People with Learning Disabilities. At: www.mentalhealth.org.uk.

Trudgill, P and Hannah, J (2013) *International English: A Guide to Varieties of Standard English*. London: Routledge.

Turney, D, Platt, D, Selwyn, J and Farmer, E (2011) *Social Work Assessment of Children in Need: What Do We Know?* Messages from Research, Department of Education.

Wastell, D and White, S (2014) Making sense of complex electronic records: socio-technical design in social care, *Applied Ergonomics*, 45(2): 143–9.

White, S, Wastell, D, Broadhurst, K and Hall, C (2010) When policy o'erleaps itself: the "tragic tale" of the integrated children's system, *Critical Social Policy*, 30(3): 405–29.

Writing in Professional Social Work Practice (2020) At: http://www.writinginsocialwork.com/ (accessed 17 June 2010).

Writing in Professional Social Work e Resources (WiSPeR) (2020) At: http://wisper.writinginsocialwork.com/ (accessed 11 August 2020).

Youth Justice Board (2020) *Making It Count in Court: Guidance and Toolkit*. At: https://yjresource-hub.uk/court-and-sentences/item/665-making-it-count-in-court-guidance-and-toolkit-yjb-2020.html (accessed 16 October 2020).

Index

Added to a page number 'f' denotes a figure and 't' denotes a table.

non-traditional students 13
normative value, of disclosure 68
Northern Ireland, professional standards 33
Northern Ireland Social Care
    Council (NISCC) 33
note-taking 37, 38f, 55
novelists 19
numerical grades 9
numerical skills 173

objectivity 15–16
OFSTED 101
online journals 87
online resources, evaluating 91–93
Open Access 87
Open University 34, 91
opinion(s) 88, 112–113
organisation
    of portfolios 76–77
    of services, knowledge and understanding
        169–170

paragraphs 51
Parker, J. 88, 93
partnership working 101
    see also working with others
pass/fail assignments 9
passive voice *see* third person writing
past tense 16
pathos 128, 148, 149
PebblePad ix, 79
peer review 49, 77, 89
Pennebaker, J.W. 154
personal development planning (PDP) 77
personal development skills 173
personal experiences *see* experiences
personal space, in portfolio systems 79
personal voice, in writing 133–134
personalisation 135
persuasive writing 58, 128–132, 147–151
plagiarism 39, 56
plans/planning
    essay writing 51, 55
    preparation for writing 38
poetry therapy 154
portfolios 71
    assessment 75, 76
    clarity and organisation 76–77
    confidentiality 80–81
    evidence included in 74–75, 78
    purpose 73–74
    weightiness of paper-based 78
    see also e-portfolios
positivist research 85
power 132, 151
practice assessment 31, 32

practice assessment reports 74, 75, 76
practice competence
    assessment as a judgement of 31
    portfolios as a demonstration of 73–74
    reflective writing as evidence of 71
    responsibility for evidence demonstrating 75
practice learning 14, 31, 71, 72
practice studies 60, 88t
practice-focused writing 71–81
    challenge/demands of 15, 16
    context 18
    drawing on theory 72–73
    portfolios *see* portfolios
    reasons for 72
    using CAPS in 24–25
pre-sentence reports 141, 146
present tense 16, 160
private law 141
problem solving 31
problem-solving 170–171
process recording 61, 62, 160–161, 162–163t
process of writing, impact of 153
Professional Capabilities
    Framework (PCF) 33, 74, 165–166
professional development 77, 79, 89, 173
professional journals 87, 88t
professional judgement
    in application of evidence/theory 89
    in case recording 110
    in report writing 127
    writing for court 139, 147–148
professional standards 33–34, 74, 88, 91, 100, 101
professional 'therapy' 61
professional views 112–113, 118,
    126, 132, 150, 151
professional voice 133, 134
professionalisation 88–89
PROMPT 91–93
providers, case recording systems 102t
psychoanalytic theory 60
psychoanalytic-based therapy 60
public law 141
published research 87, 89
purpose 20–21
    academic writing 24
    case recording 105t, 106t
    practice writing 25
    reflective writing 66t
    report writing 122, 123
    writing up research 94t
'Putting People First' 135

qualitative research 85
Quality Assurance Agency (QAA) 30, 32–33, 34
Quality Care Commission 101
quality control, books and journals 91